Prayer Beads on the Train

Another Collection of Stories Written on the MTA

By Anne Born

You might also like
A Marshmallow on the Bus:
A Collection of Stories Written on the MTA
By Anne Born

ISBN-13:978-1500164379
The Backpack Press
March 2015

Dedicated to the memory
of the extraordinary women in my family:
Annie, Alice, Belle, Dot, Gracie, Nannie,
Dot, Doll, Nita, Marge, and Diane;
Charlotte, Mary Emma, Bessie, Clara Mae,
Dorothy, Esther, and Helen

Contents

For once you have tasted flight
you will walk the earth with your eyes turned skywards,
for there you have been
and there you will long to return.

~Leonardo da Vinci

Introduction

I feel a bit like the rock band that puts out a first album everyone enjoys and then is faced with following it up with something equally enjoyable. Sophomore efforts are criticized – lots – and it makes me wonder how anyone ever gets the second opus out in the sunlight. But here it is: my sophomore effort.

While the stories in my first collection, *A Marshmallow on the Bus*, were about the train, the bus, the view from my bus shelter, *Prayer Beads on the Train,* named after a train story in *Marshmallow*, is more about memory and loss, memoir and family, my view while sitting on the train or the bus. I have added a number of short fiction pieces and some new poetry.

I am indebted to my new Queens literary community for support, encouragement, and camaraderie – all of which this writer needed. Special thanks to the *Newtown Literary Journal*, Valerie for *Poetry & Coffee*, Aida for *Boundless Tales*, Kambri at Q.E.D Astoria, and with much love to Mike and Marvin with *Inspired Word.* Outside Queens, sincere thanks to Dane and Sabrina for *Local Poets*, Eric for *Word Up*, Julia for the New York Transit Museum *Platform Series*, Jonathan for *Passionate Justice*, Bridget and the *Five Boro Story Project*, Joanne and *The Broad Side*, and Matt at *Hostel Geeks* – I am indeed proud to know you all. And Meryl Marcus at Columbia.

I'd like to thank Nina and my NYC Pilgrims, and Padre Alexis at Blessed Sacrament Church in Manhattan for being so supportive of my writing about the Camino de Santiago. And Jason for helping me cover my books.

My family also has been so very patient with me as I find my voice – both in print and in spoken word. I have to thank Charlie, Mike, Mary, Lucy, Grace, and now, Ben, for giving me the space and encouragement I needed to work and the pier to which I might tether my little boat.

As always, I hope you enjoy my little bus stories.

In Just Spring

Spring is a sketchy business where I come from. It comes and goes with the day, one day warm, one day cool again, like a boat trying to right itself in choppy water. Then you can wake up on some random Tuesday and not even see that thc boat is under full sail, gliding out across a calm sea. By the time you notice, you're there, you've reached summer, and that fluffy, light as air "just spring" is gone.

So, how is it that with as many springs as I've seen in my life, do I still find it hard to stay warm? I am never as cold as I am in the spring. It's in the low 50s, but I am convinced that winter is over so I wear something fresh and I find myself, waiting for the bus, digging my hands into my pockets and burying my face in my collar to stay warm. I wrap up in blankets on my couch because I can't bring myself to close the windows. And I am still making hot chocolate and feeling sorry for myself that I cannot shake the chill.

If it's in the low 50s in October, you know to put on something warm, so you pull out the fleecy things and it's part of the "look." You think of football games instead of baseball games and everyone in the stands wears hoods and mittens. If it's in the low 50s in January, it's a heat wave and the gloves come off just long enough to make you think of the warm days to come. So why is it, when it's in the low 50s in April, I never seem to get the wardrobe right, year after year? And why is it the same temperature feels so different at different times of the year? Is it me, or is it some dastardly meteorological plot?

It's sunny today in New York, and tomorrow, it's supposed to be in the low 50s. I have my winter jacket and a toasty sweater so I can go out and enjoy spring. I might even join *bettyandisbel* when they *come dancing*. It is, as e.e. cummings would say, "just spring," after all, and it doesn't last, whether you freeze your way through it or not.

It's a frothy dessert, best served outdoors.

Eternity in an Hour

Do you wear a watch? I do. I'm not always on time just because I wear a watch, but I do like to know what time it is without having to ask someone. Part habit, part throw-back, part old lady, I guess, but knowing the time is a comfort to me.

In my family, great events are acknowledged by gifts of timepieces. My great-grandfather's gift to his bride in 1896 was an austere black mantel clock with a maddening tick-tock and sonorific hourly chime. It sat in our basement for decades after they died, because the noise was like Poe's "tintinnabulation that so musically wells"; nobody knowing what to do with it, and, at the same time, nobody wanting to part with it either. It's not particularly rare or street-valuable, but to me, there's magic in the idea that he wanted her to think of him when she looked at the clock. It sits in my living room now, on my bookcase.

My dad gave me my mother's gold watch, after she died. Its value to me is in my memory of her wearing it. It never fit her slim wrist and she was constantly shifting it around so she could see the face. I can see her so clearly when I look at that watch.

When I graduated from high school, I got a watch. It's in a drawer now but I keep it because it reminds me of my high school self, so focused on the day at hand and not thinking once of the day out in front of me. My mother wanted me to know the make, I remember that, so I would appreciate the value, but I can't remember the name without looking at it now. And because I would have to wind it each night for it to keep time all day, it's not something I will ever wear. My current watch is mostly plastic and runs on a battery I replace every year.

I remember the famous Biltmore clock. Now, that was a clock. You would say, "Meet me under the Biltmore clock," and you would never worry that people couldn't find you. It was a tall street clock that stood outside the Biltmore

Hotel in Manhattan. When they demolished the hotel in 1981, I read that the clock was moved indoors to the lobby of the new building. But now, with cellphones, you can meet people anywhere you like on a moment's notice and the phone will tell you the time too.

My grandfather sweated time. He worked as a streetcar operator in Chicago when he was younger and was always so afraid of being late that he was at the door, hat in hand, with 15 to 20 minutes to spare whenever we were going out. If he were ever late to his shift, he would have jeopardized the schedule and relieving the other driver. I think that streetcar line was lucky to have him.

I got a "new" clock over the weekend when I was home visiting my family. It is one of a set of twin clocks that were owned by my mother and her sister. This one, a lovely white ceramic mantel clock with shiny black trim, came with the winding key, the one thing I was missing from that wedding clock.

I want to wind the wedding clock tonight and see if I can set that tick-tock on its way. I probably won't make it past the noise of the first chiming, but I want to hear it and get a sense again of how it worked when it was new. I imagine my great-grandmother as a newlywed, centering it on her mantel, in their first house, without the constant noise of television, or keyboard strokes, and without the overhead sounds of jet engines or the clicking of stop lights and traffic on the street. That soft and constant ticking, that was so irritating to me when I was younger, would have been the background to the cries of my grandmother as a baby or the celebratory singing of carols at Christmas.

Maybe, if I can get it going, I'll be able to hear some of that as well. After all, it's about time.

A Home for Clouds

Don't you ever ask them why, if they told you, you would cry,
*So just look at them and sigh and know they love you.**

On a flight into New York recently, I was fortunate to sit in front of a wonderful dad and his inquisitive son. Dad was in the middle seat, son by the window where he had the standard view of lots of clouds.

I have to be honest, I was more than a little apprehensive sitting just in front of these two because I was sure the kid was going to whine, or kick the seat, or start any of the other irritating things strangers' kids do on planes.

I flew a lot with my own children when they were that age and it was not pleasant. They would be fine until we got on the plane. Then, they dropped the cute kid traveler act that beguiled the flight attendants as we boarded, and reverted to crying, lots of general fussing, followed by a coma-like sleep that would set in about five minutes before we landed, making it near impossible to get them off the plane.

But this was different in a fascinating way. The boy liked looking at the clouds out the window. His dad was encouraging, bringing out the budding scientist in the boy. They were engaging each other and I couldn't stop myself from eavesdropping.

"Why are the clouds moving slower than the plane?" the boy asked his dad.

"The plane has to move pretty fast to stay up in the air," the dad responded.

Boy: "Where are the clouds going?"

Dad: "Where do you think? You know, some days aren't cloudy at all."

Boy: "Are they going home?"

Dad: "Where's home?"

Boy: "Do they die on the ground? Do they become water?"

Dad: "Yes, yes, that's it."

Boy: "I got it right!"

Superficially, I applauded this conversation because the dad did not give his son the answer or laugh when he thought the clouds might be going home – like *they* were. But the more important message to me was how, when left to ponder and to mull, when left to discern and to think, this boy came up with a very plausible answer all on his own.

It was a small, sweet wonder.

*Graham Nash, *Teach Your Children*

Zebras in the Foyer

There's a Benjamin Moore paint store on Lexington Avenue that used to have samples of the iconic Scalamandre wallpaper in the display window. I'd go by and imagine I was the kind of hip, city guy who could Scalamandre a wall or two and when people came in for a cucumber sandwich, they'd nod knowingly and I'd be in their club.

I pictured myself getting off the 6 train at 68th Street and walking in there, gesturing to the wallpaper salesperson with the back of my hand, saying, "Yes, hello, I'm interested in some paper, please." I'd select the dancing zebras in that exquisite blood red, and I'd take a swatch with me because I'd want someone to do matching throw pillows for the imaginary settee next to my Chinese armoire in my imaginary foyer. I'd want many.

Of course, bona fide club members never shop for themselves. I know that. They have people. Oh hell, their *people* have people and none of them take the 6 train. And they probably don't sweat the Two Large it's going to cost just to order one roll and have it hung. My real foyer isn't all that big.

I did wallpaper once – above the wood paneling in my dining room. It was blue Toile and I loved it. But if I'm going to be honest, I got it because it was the only wall space in my apartment that was beyond the reach of my four children. I wanted that club thing. I wanted to have people say, "I love what you've done here," with a swishy kind of back and forth hand gesture so I'd know they meant the wallpaper.

But I just can't let the dancing zebras go just yet. I sit on my couch imagining an accent wall of zebras or a full on dining room full of zebras. I could put them in the kitchen or the big bathroom.

Still, I worry it will make me poor and make my house look, well, like Club El Morocco. Is that a bad thing?

A Third of Your Life or FOMO?

Most mornings, I run the TV in the background while I make breakfast and get ready for work. Sometimes I sit and stare, not taking much in, and sometimes I get interested in a story and I'll pay a little more attention. For some reason, a mattress ad caught my attention this morning. It claimed that since we all spend a third of our lives sleeping, one's choice of mattress should matter.

Really? A third of our lives? Whoever calculated that number most definitely was not a New York mother.

I stopped sleeping for eight hours a night when I was pregnant with my oldest daughter, my first child. Even though my four pregnancies were fairly easy with only minor distractions, I quickly gave up a "full night's sleep," as the mattress company describes. Either I couldn't find a comfortable angle, or I was too hot, too cold, too something. I would sleep in bits, staying awake long enough to worry about twinges, worry about being awake certainly, or worry about how we were going to like having a baby.

Then, after the baby moved in, she couldn't make it for eight hours either and we would both be up, sleeping in bits. I would sing and rock her for the longest time between 2:00 and 4:00 a.m. most nights. I learned all the words to a handful of my mother's favorite songs from the 1940s Hit Parade and even though I wasn't getting nearly enough sleep, those fabulous late nights singing with my baby more than made up for it. I was exhausted, but happy.

Fast forward to her siblings' appearances and the nighttime ritual of singing plus rocking went on for years, not one year of which did I ever get eight hours' sleep. I found myself learning more about the night in the process and becoming intrigued that life did go on, every single night, even though other people were sleeping. It started to remind me of children's books that I loved where whole cities of elves or trolls or demons lived out of sight of the mortals they would annoy, and *In the Night Kitchen* became one of my favorite books to read at bedtime.

When the babies were a bit older, I took a job as a typesetter at an all-night copy shop where I would design business cards, newsletters, and fliers for all the night owls on the Upper West Side of Manhattan. Guys in neighboring bars would come in to see if we could make cards for them that said they were movie producers or high-end stockbrokers so they could flash them around and pick up girls. Those nights, I would sleep from 4:00 a.m. until it was time to take the kids to school, with a late afternoon nap to catch up. More bits.

And now that my babies are all twenty-somethings, I wake up when they come in late from work or dates with their friends. I have an uncanny way of waking up at the precise moment they approach our door. It's like there is some force field that alerts me they are coming in even though I don't let on I'm awake.

So, a third of my life sleeping? Most definitely not! And even though I no longer check on them to see if they are still breathing, I still feel like the night watchman. I think it probably tips them a little off balance when I send them Tweets or texts at 3:45 a.m., but it's only because I am a mom who just doesn't need to spend a third of her life sleeping.

You know, I can't even say that would be a goal because of a recently identified ailment called FOMO, the "Fear Of Missing Out." I consider myself lucky that New York is an up-all-night kind of place. So, I guess what started as a mom thing has morphed into a FOMO thing.

After all, I could miss something!

But, you know, now that I think about it, a new mattress still might be nice. I use my bed to sort clothes and organize my bills, magazines, catalogs, papers, subscriptions, travel plans, and I, and, and I, zzzzzzzzzzzz ...

Christmas in My Kitchen

When I was little, we had a couple of Christmas traditions that I still think are pretty swell. We had a fresh-cut tree, my dad would string lights around the front door, and piles of presents would miraculously appear on Christmas morning. My sister and I could select our favorite toy to take along to Mass and we'd drive away to spend time with my mother's family in Chicago where we could visit with my cousins. There would be a big dinner and we had that one aunt who always nipped a little too much and sang. My mother would say something about the Irish and drinking and we'd come home to play with the toys we'd left under the tree. And there was snow. Lots of snow.

I moved away from my family when I was still in graduate school and I had to establish my own Christmas priorities pretty early on. I wasn't always able to go home and I wasn't always *interested* in going home. I loved my family and I think they loved me, but sometimes I would spend Christmas someplace else. For starters, that meant picking my own time to go to Mass. I could be daring and go to Midnight Mass or I could be retro and wait for High Mass in the morning. This meant I was also free to decide when "Christmas Dinner" was and where. My being able to make all of these decisions myself made me dizzy with glee.

Early on, I sang Midnight Mass in the church choir. That had a wonderful impact on my holiday because I could share the music, the exhaustion of trying to perform at that hour, and the difficulty trying to find cabs to get home from churches in so-so neighborhoods where you didn't want to be waiting on a subway platform at 2:00 a.m. That meant dinner could be early on Christmas Eve or Christmas Day, or both for that matter, and it was fun. Sometimes we'd have a nice traditional dinner and then go out for Chinese on Christmas Day, sipping free white wine and dipping dumplings while we watched the snow fall outside the window of the restaurant.

When I had children, we were obligated to go to their grandmother's house and the decisions started to withdraw slowly from my hands and appear in hers. Since she staged a very nice event every year, it was never a burden just to go along. I still sang, but dinner was "up in the country," as New Yorkers say, meaning anything more than a mile out of town.

And then my children and I left home to make our own way in our own apartment and all those great bits and pieces of the holiday came flooding back to me. Sing, or not sing? Most times, I sang. Dinner before or after? We picked Chinese. Tree or no tree was a difficult one at first, because I felt that I might be betraying some requisite tradition if I decided not to have one at all. Trees can run over $100 in New York, so there were more than a few Christmases when I just couldn't afford it and still have money to buy presents.

We started to downsize the holiday altogether and I replaced the big green fresh-cut tree with a table-sized one. That's how my favorite new tradition began. Since that first tree was roughly the height of my youngest daughter, she believed I had selected it for that reason. So, every tree since, in the years when we weren't traveling, the tree has been her height. She's about 5' 4" now, but we're traveling this Christmas and probably won't have a tree this year. If we do, I will take her with me to determine its perfect size.

My mother had a beautiful ceramic Nativity set that had a great little baby Jesus with the expected animals and bit players - and I loved it. Dollhouses were my constant toys as a kid, so arranging and rearranging the religious pieces to create just the right ensemble scene was my favorite part.

My older daughter brought me a Nativity set from Spain last year, so I have the key personnel now and I have been adding little "guys," as I call them, from each of my trips. I added a tiny Tango couple from my trip to Argentina, a chubby little bull fighter, some crazy-eyed Flamenco dancers from my own trips to Spain, and a little black rooster from Portugal. Just like the collection of antique family tree ornaments my mother had for our trees, I can add little "guys" to this set every time I come back from a trip and then next year's holiday will reflect my travels. It doesn't take up too much room, it doesn't cost anything much, and it doesn't make me worry about that drying fresh-cut tree if we travel and aren't around much over Christmas.

And it all fits on top of the microwave – which is where it is sitting right now. I call it: "Christmas in my Kitchen."

Boots

Winter this year has brought a lot of snow into our lives. New Yorkers got used to not having it for so long, it's almost like a surprise when the forecast calls for some inches of snowfall. Today we were supposed to be visited by what meteorologists call a Classic Nor'easter. It was going to drop 30 inches of snow on the city tonight and the prospect of all that snow started to sound pretty dire. Then, mid-week, the weather people all backed off and re-calibrated the inches in their forecast to a mere tenth of the original estimate. As I write, it hasn't started snowing yet, but odds are we'll only see a dusting. What that means is simply this: no boots.

Sidewalks and most streets in New York are cleared of snow in a way that I do not remember streets getting clean when I was growing up in Michigan. I remember walking through streets that had not been plowed where the snow was measured more accurately in feet than in inches. And I wore boots all the time. My mother would cut off sheets of wax paper for me to wrap up my stockinged feet so they would slide into my boots. It would get all wet when the snow came over the tops of my boots, but everyone had wax paper so soggy socks just became part of the deal.

Except for my dad. My dad had a regular boot protocol too. It was more efficient and less necessary at the same time. More efficient, because the way he would tuck his pants' cuffs into his boots made it virtually impossible for snow to get into his socks and less necessary, because he drove a car everywhere and rarely walked any great distance in the snow. He would shovel out the driveway every time it snowed of course, but his feet followed the shovel he pushed ahead of him and he walked on the clear ground left by the path.

But every time I pull on my snow boots now, I think about my dad and his boots. They were dark, thick rubber boots, about 10 inches tall with a center front gusset and two big tin buckles. He would sit in the kitchen with the boots next to him on the floor. Then he would carefully fold his pants' cuffs around his ankles so they lay flat on his socks. Like hospital corners on bed sheets, his neatly folded pants fit perfectly into his boots. The gusset would close and lay flat too so the buckles would make everything close up tight and everything was neat.

Watching my dad perform this simple procedure made me feel safe. Regardless of how imperfect my own boot application was on any given day, I thought if my dad could do this with such precision, it must mean that he did other things with equal thought and experience and knowledge. He knew how to make sure no snow got in his boots and I was always coming home with wet socks. He had neat buckles and creased pants and I had wax paper. I had something to aspire to, something to assign to being a grown-up. Kids got wet socks, grown-ups had that all solved.

My dad stays indoors most of the time now and I'm not sure he still has the boots I remember. When I bought the ones I wear in the New York slush now, I tried to find something practical like the ones he used to wear. I got short Wellies that do the job and I make sure I take the time to fold my pants across my ankles the way he did. I take the extra step of pulling my stretchy socks over the hems to make sure everything is snug because, after all, that's what grown-ups do.

Last week, I was wearing the boots on my way in from the train station when I came up to a stretch of blocked sidewalk that forced me to walk out into the street, around the car that was pulled over the path. I took one step out to the street and stepped into deep water that had puddled against the curb and the slush went up nearly to the top of my boots, roughly eight inches. But my feet were still dry! I started laughing out loud at how clever I was to have worn my boots and to have dry socks.

But it was all my dad, and I have to be honest: I started to feel like a grown-up.

Canes

Lately, I've been noticing people with canes. I understand how useful they can be if you have injured your foot, your leg, for instance. Use a cane while it heals.

But the canes I have been watching are being used by older people. Typically, they are not pretty or decorated. They look worn and they bow sometimes from supporting the weight of their owner. At every other step, there is something to hang onto, to lean on, to use to keep your balance.

I wonder what the first day is like with a cane.

At my bus stop, there is a wonderful woman who waits for buses with me nearly every morning. We're both older than most of our compatriots on the bus and like many older people, we worry about tomorrow a lot more than we let on. She and I grouse about the bus drivers and we keep tabs on other regular riders.

Something she said to me once has bothered me since it first came up months ago. We were talking about walking home from the office in a power outage. We agreed it would be an effort to cover this distance on foot and she told me suddenly, "You know, I'd hate to have to start using a cane. I want to hold out to the last minute."

We both walk now unaided and many days, I will go out of my way to find nice walks because walking clears my head. In fact, I know that I could walk the entire route to my office more often if I had the organizational skills necessary to get out of the house a half hour to forty-five minutes earlier. She, on the other hand, might not be as comfortable, even though she clearly does not need a cane. Today.

But how do you know it's time? Is there something that cries out to you that today is the day you surrender to old age and start using a cane? Does a doctor tell you to use one? Or is this something that creeps up where you just don't remember later how it started, how you found yourself in the store, picking out a cane?

I can't imagine they would be any harder to get used

to than my new hiking poles. I took them out for a spin and had the rhythm down pat in just a few steps. If the height is right and the feel of the handle doesn't irritate your hand, how difficult would it be to use a cane? It'd be pretty simple, right? Step, cane-step; step, cane-step; step, cane-step. And off you go.

But then, there's no going back, is there? Now you are officially a senior citizen, an older American, a what, disabled person? With that one stroke, you would go from being able to disabled and unlike the ones who use canes when they have sustained an injury, you will know, deep down, there's no going back to normal. You don't get to improve or get better. This is the moment you would have to realize you can only get less better. Today, cane; tomorrow, walker? Then, wheelchair? And those beautiful shiny black hiking poles that were so exciting the first time out, will be left in the closet for someone else to use. Someone younger.

I am not ready to give up hiking just yet. I want to walk unaided and I relish every single chance I get to do so. Of course, I worry this walk today or maybe one tomorrow could be the one where I realize I just can't do it anymore. It's too hard or I worry too much that I could fall.

But, I hope it's not this walk. It's almost sunset now and the breeze is amazing. I feel it on my face and when I step out, it nudges me forward. I stretch up to my full height at each street corner and I step carefully across all those cracks in the sidewalk. I catch a glimpse of kids on the swings, the men playing dominoes at the card tables alongside the vegetable market, and the young girls comparing notes on that boy across the street. I don't want to miss any of this – this wonderful and exuberant life of the city – and it's fabulous that nobody even notices me as I walk by.

As I walk by.

God, I love those words.

Six Glass Plates

It was almost 20 years ago and Woolworth's was going out of business. My children were small and we were moving out, moving on, moving up, but we didn't have much, so my friends pitched in, donating kitchen things, bedroom things, bathroom things. We got a bacon grabber from one, a trunk load of groceries from two others, and I found out just how wonderful my friends were because before I knew I needed something, someone was already there, helping us out.

With few resources beyond that, I shopped the Woolworth's closeouts and the 99 cent stores. I bought pots and pans and six glass plates. There would be one each for the five of us and one for a guest in case someone needed dinner, I guess, even though at the time, we were sharing cans of Chef Boyardee. The plates were made out of glass with an abstract design on the border and some small fleur de lys, and I paid 99 cents apiece for them. To me, they were an achievement, a statement. I could buy my own plates and they weren't awful or ugly. And they weren't hand-me-down either. They were mine. When I set the table for dinner, such as it was in those early days, the plates became my own declaration of independence. We didn't have much, but the plates said we were going to be OK.

To be fair, I don't remember ever taking extra care with them. I think, on some level, I expected things would improve, and ultimately, I planned to replace them. We didn't have a dishwasher then, so I must have washed them each by hand over a thousand times and they survived my four children and all that washing and came through without a scratch.

Our finances did improve over time and I was able to buy new plates with a sketch of the New York skyline on them, but we kept setting the table for dinner with the glass plates. They had become something of a tradition in a house that had few traditions. When we finally moved out of that first apartment a few years ago, we took the glass plates with us even though we could have donated them to the church with a lot of our other early kitchen things. I could have put them up on a top shelf in my new kitchen, but for some reason, they stayed in use, and nearly every day, someone uses one of the glass plates.

A few months ago, I broke one. I had set it down in the sink and accidentally tipped something hot against it and it cracked in two. I thought, well, we have five more and there's still just the five of us and we have the skyline plates now. But last night, another one cracked. I was getting ready to load our new dishwasher and saw the crack along the edge, running underneath the border.

I have a few choices now. I can put the remaining plates up on a shelf and forget about them. They'll stay safe, but out of sight. I could make some kind of artful display and leave them out in the open, but I'm really not one for the artful display of dinner plates. Or I could just keep using them, knowing full well that someone will probably break the rest of them, one by one, and the glass plates will finally be gone.

So, as you might have guessed, I have to opt for use over storage. I love these plates and I still want to see them every day. They came into our lives as a six-dollar, kitchen supply purchase and became a tradition. The glass plates are a measure of how far we've come from the days when my friends gave us their bacon grabber and bought us groceries.

I hope everyone will forgive me if I have to make an artful display of the last one.

New Day

Nothing clears the air
like walking in front of a sanitation truck
sitting idling on the Concourse,
as I head for the train in the morning

Nothing prepares me for my day
like seeing a baseball-capped young man leapfrog
over a fire hydrant
and just about lose his pants.

Or the sound of the subway turnstiles
screaming back at me when I swipe through,
the sticky touch of the handrails
when I cross over the platforms
to get to my next train.

Nothing cleanses the palette
the way hot lattes do when they burn my mouth
after I've ignored the "this beverage is extremely hot"
warning on the side of the white paper cup.

And yet, now that I am sufficiently refreshed,
I can begin the whole process again
and keep going,
as I head for the train in the morning.

The taste of clean air now,
rushes down the escalator as I skim up to the street.

The snap of a free newspaper
and the tang of fresh printer's ink
singes the inside of my nose.
Sunlight smacks the shiny sides of the elevated train
on its way into Queens.

The shadow on the wall is larger than that old tree –
it's like graffiti writ'n across gray concrete,
down the block from the guy
sweeping the street in front of the Chinese place.

I just keep moving.

Cleanse the palette again and again.
Take it all in and swirl it around
again and again and again.

New York is an acquired taste
like olives,
or peppers with salt.
It's Jameson's one day, Diet Coke the next.
It's hot dogs in the morning,
and pizza at night,
familiar today,
brand spanking new tomorrow.

I like to watch where I'm going,
Moving oh so carefully up the street,
As I head for the train in the morning.

Wearing Fiction

Sitting at the Detroit Metro Airport last week, I couldn't help noticing the young man sitting right next to me, waiting for a flight. It was around 30 degrees outside, not untypical for Detroit in January and we were flying to northern Indiana. He was wearing flip-flops. Bare feet and flip-flops.

So, I ask you, what was he trying to communicate to his audience by wearing something so completely inappropriate and accompanying them with a heavy winter coat and a long preppy scarf?

This must be his fiction.

He probably gets up in the morning and pulls items of clothing from his wardrobe with the idea that whatever he puts together will speak about him without words. I am guessing he believes that we all will draw some quick conclusions about his devil-may-care insouciance. Did I mention he was also wearing a Bass Pro Shop hat?

It's not that I begrudge him his display and I certainly will allow that he might not have thought about shoes when he stepped out of the house that morning on his way to the airport. But here's the thing: I think he was just broadcasting his own great story of him. Flip-Flop Guy is not unlike me wishing I could buy more khaki so that people will think I'm more daring than I really am. He's like a young woman I used to know who swathed herself in Kente cloth, hoping people would think she was really from Africa when we all knew she grew up in Baltimore. I used to wonder if the fiction she maintained was ever a burden for her or if she woke up sometimes and wished she could just jump into a tee-shirt and jeans and call it a day.

Tee-shirt and jeans is actually a great equalizer but try wearing a completely plain shirt and regular jeans and you will see what retail is trying to tell you about these simple, American staples. Tee-shirts have sayings, designs, logos, slogans like "We are the 99%." Jeans have designers and special rivets and colors and stretch. So there really is very little to choose from that doesn't say something.

Writing a full blown fictional character is something we do every time we get dressed in the morning. In my house, I have dark pants that I think look more professional than jeans certainly, and I like simple, non-distracting colors because I am in customer service and I like not to stand out when I am trying to keep the focus on everyone else. But to be fair, I have seen what my colleagues wear and I try to look like them. I don't spend too much thought on it either, but when I shop for clothes, I keep collecting things that make me look my age, I guess, and are suitable. Suitable is a very big word in the business world and I do want people to take me seriously, even before I say anything.

So what would happen if I were to go a little more khaki? What if I abandoned the dark pants for the ones that zip off at the knees? Would I be tempted to follow my fiction and really do something more adventurous? Could I really become more daring? I like to think so. I want to believe that the only thing standing between me and that globe trekker lady on Channel 13 is the wardrobe, that I am just as brave and daring as she is and I just need the khaki pants, oatmeal-flecked wool socks, and hiking boots. And maybe a jaunty hat or some flip-flops.

Now that's fiction. And as long as I'm making it up every day, I think I'm going to want those zip-off pants by the time I get to Chapter Two.

Confessions of a Travel Junkie

It's time to come clean. New year, new day, nothing to hide, no looking back, right?

I am a travel junkie.

Oh my, that feels better already.

My guess is you all knew this before I did. You were kind, didn't want to say something that might set me off and damage our friendship. You made sure you were not enabling my habit by sending me colorful postcards of places you'd been or condoning my behavior in any way. And you probably were content just to mention something to someone at the dinner table, something like, "She's at it again. I just don't know what to say or when she'll be back."

So, let me lay my cards on this virtual table. I have a habit. Like other people who wait for shoes to go on sale, I stalk airplane tickets. I have alerts sent to my E-mail box that let me know when to fly, when to buy, where to go next. When I buy the paper, I go to the business section first because business people fly more often than the rest of us. And you'd think that one important distinction, my not being a business person as opposed to others who are doing business, would stop me, but it doesn't. I have ways, protocols, tricks. I know how to get in and out clean at Expedia Dot Com. They know me there. I feel welcome. They remember where I've gone.

It started simply enough. You could say I wasn't even looking for a new habit. There was a woman who had an office next to mine about ten years ago. We had a long holiday weekend here where I work and she came in to say she and her husband were going to Barcelona for the weekend. "Really? Barcelona in Spain? And just for the weekend?" She said, "Yes," or "¡Sí!" I don't remember. They flew out on Thursday evening, arrived Friday morning, did lots of cool Barcelona things all day Friday, Saturday, and Sunday, and flew back to JFK mid-afternoon on Monday.

She would be back in the office on Tuesday. And she was not a business person.

That was it. I was transfixed. She had just given me the license to bug out to Barcelona any time I wanted. This one small conversation opened the door for me just to go to the nearest airport and travel. I started with a trip to Paris. I scouted airfares, picked the cheapest days to travel, rented an apartment from a friend, and took off. Then it was Seville. Same protocol. Scouting, picking, renting, taking off. After that, it was the Bahamas and Bermuda, lots more Paris and Spain, and then Morocco, Ireland, Portugal, Argentina, Uruguay. God, I get high just thinking of this!

My best fix ever was on a Wednesday afternoon in October 2010. I was in my office, cruising around on Expedia just to keep body and soul together, and I found I could fly, yes, to Barcelona, the next day for an impossibly low fare. (I kind of know all the current fares to my favorite places by heart). I bought it, I flew the next day, met up with my daughter who was living in Spain at the time, and we shopped, ate, saw Flamenco, ate more, walked on the beach, and I came home on Monday. No, make that I came home on Monday, exhilarated and happy.

I know a good bit of this comes from my not traveling anywhere much when I was a kid growing up nowhere near an airport. We went on two family trips together when I was in grade school, I went to Mexico once in high school, and I spent Thanksgiving in Toronto once in college. Other than that, I was in graduate school before I visited my fourth U.S. state and I was 30 when I applied for my first passport.

So, it's something I don't want to give up, this need to get out of town. I live in a pretty wonderful town, too. Yet, for all of this travel, I don't feel like an expert in anything more than how to afford to do it, my not being a business person and all. I know that my four trusting children, who drag along after me, know more about the world than I did in my many years of going to only three states.

So, I could say I do this for the kids, but this is a confession after all, so I will stick to the truth. I travel because it thrills me. I shun fear and pack my backpack and I take off. And then, I plot how I can do it again. I guess I just go from fix to fix.

You won't tell anyone else, will you?

Come, come, whoever you are.
Wanderer, worshiper, lover of leaving. It doesn't matter.
Ours is not a caravan of despair.
Come, even if you have broken your vows a thousand times.
Come, yet again, come, come.

Jelaluddin Rumi (1207-1273)

My Spanish Rooster

I spent three weeks living in northwest Spain in 2014, volunteering in an office that means a lot to me. I was housed in a beautiful house, cared for by the nicest people, and for the most part, I was left alone. But every morning, the neighborhood rooster woke me up and it forced me to examine how similar - or dissimilar - I am to a rooster.

To begin with, roosters are guys. I like to think of myself as a "guy" but I'm really a girl. I can't say I identify with chickens and it's been decades since anyone called me a chick, so I guess I walk away from this detail and keep moving.

Roosters get up early. You know, I like to get up early too because I can be assured that the house will be quiet and I can make my coffee without distractions or company. Once I have my coffee, you can sit and we can talk - but not before, please. I need that water pouring, that filter finding, and that coffee measuring to happen in silence so I can concentrate and not screw it all up. Once that is in place, my day can start.

Roosters strut. They walk around like they own the place. I don't do that much. I tend to keep my head down - so much so that once when I was hiking in the mountains with my son, he had to remind me to take in the view.

And roosters crow. I'm a city girl - always have been - so I don't have all that much experience with roosters, but they make that noise every morning. And they don't quit really - lots of roosters crow well into the afternoon. This particular Spanish rooster had an uncanny way of knowing when I was up, fed, dressed, and ready to leave. That's when *El Gallo* stopped crowing.

So I wonder how it is this smallish bird can go from quiet, listening to the other littler birds chirping in the trees, to full-blown screeching at the incredible decibel levels that I heard every day. How does anyone go from full quiet to air-splitting noise? And is there no other way for the rooster to get his message across?

I can't do that.

If it's quiet, I respect the quiet. If it's noisy, I long for quiet. I cannot imagine bridging the gap between existing quiet and full-on screeching. I suppose that's a flaw, that I should pipe up more, keep my head down less, make more noise. But I don't. I used to. But now I don't.

So, I envy the rooster. He got up every day before I did and experienced a tiny bit of Galicia that I never saw - the pre-rooster crowing dawn. Still, I am happy to have heard him have his say in Spain and now, just to enjoy the traffic noise that wakes me up these days in the Bronx. Once in a while, I will hear some little birds in the trees outside my window too and remember that nervy rooster.

I doubt he'd remember me.

To The Woman

To the woman who walked ahead of me
on the way to the train this morning:
I was doing just fine til I saw you.
I left the house, smiling at the new day
Inhaling the first fresh air, listening to the birds.
Then you came up from behind me,
Crossed into my path ahead of me
on the way to the "D" train
And every sweet bit of my day
Screeched to a halt
As I caught sight,
Isn't that what they say?
Caught sight?
As I caught sight of them,
Of it,
Of them and
Dear sweet merciful heavens on a sesame seed bun!
You were wearing striped underpanties
And I really didn't want to know that –
But there was your butt
Squeezed into those sheer drugstore leggings,
And I could not take my eyes off your ample ass.
It was like a speedboat making its way across a still lake
With a rippling wake, pulling me along like a water skier.
I could not look away.
And I was hit with the questions:
Who let you go out like this
Who told you to buy those pants
Where are you going
Do you live by yourself?
And since you had no rear view mirror, no friends,
No family to stop you from displaying your, dare I say,
derriere?
With your panties all there
Dragging me along with them down the street just now,

I felt bad for you.
I wanted to take you aside
Let you know I could count the stripes on your backside
But I could not for the life of me think of how to say that.
Ma'am your ass is hanging out of your pants.
Ma'am you've got striped panties on and we all see them.
Ma'am your pants are transparent
Translucent transportational transmogriphying?
I didn't say anything.
I didn't want you to hit me.
I didn't want you to ask what I was doing checking out your butt
And why didn't I just mind my own business?
After all, did I really think you'd listen to me and go home to change?
And change what? The panties? The pants?
(Wasn't I grateful she was *wearing* panties?)

Then you crossed the street and I broke free.
I got on the platform and I got on my train.

And now?
Simply this:
You will never know that today
Your ass was a speedboat dragging us all behind
your behind.

Haulin' Oates or How I Became Kindle-ized

Never one to shun electronic advancements or tiny new gadgets and toys, I tend however to wait a bit before jumping in to buy them. I cannot claim to be the first to own a personal computer, the first to use a cellphone, or the first to make home movies for the old VCR. I do tend to know about these advances ahead of the pack, but I also tend to let the pack try them out first, wait to let the micro-chips fall where they may, and then jump in. It's safer that way and I don't get stuck with a lot of Betamax tapes and no way to view them.

So when the Kindle and Nook E-readers came out, it was the same. I thought they were dumb. And I worried they spelled the end of the book, which disturbed me to no end. So it has been a long road, filled with emotional potholes stemming from my lifelong attachment to books, but, as of a few weeks ago, I am finally Kindle-ized and ironically, it was a book that pushed me into this realm of E-toy ownership and use.

I am reading *The Accursed* by Joyce Carol Oates. It's fun, it's about Princeton, it's Gothic, but the hardcover book weighs one pound, 13.9 ounces. I have been carrying it around with me every day for nearly a month and I'm done. I don't want to do this anymore. While I love the smell of a new book and the wonderful feel of the paper turning and bookmarking, I am tired of carrying the book. I want the freedom to travel light and I love that Kindle books are cheaper. I'm sold!

My kids think it's because I'm really old, that my fragile little old lady shoulders can't carry the weight of this particularly large book. That's not the whole story. Big books like this one, and all the Harry Potter books, require a particular skill in laying it down on your lap or on a table so you don't have to hold the thing in two hands while you read. *That's* what I won't miss: trying to juggle large books on the train or the bus, where I usually like to read them.

This book forced me to change my bag so I had enough space to carry it. This book, this wonderfully entertaining book, forced me to look at the way I read. And maybe it was my knowing there was a slippery slope coming if I even *tried* reading on my iPad. And that was right. Not only am I going to keep reading books with my iPad Kindle app, I already subscribe to the Wall Street Journal and two magazines. And my daughter recommended a glorious app called, of all things, Free Books. I have already downloaded a dozen books of poetry and I can read Dante any time I like without pulling the book off my shelf, finding a bag big enough, and laying it out on a table to read.

I lament the loss of marginalia with the advent of E-readers. I love when you buy used books and the previous owner has penciled in some faint *bons mots* on the bottom or the side of the page. I loved getting books in college that were already underlined, not because it saved me the work of deciding what was important, what was not, but because it built an invisible community of readers and connected me to the greater literary universe.

If it's any consolation, I do feel awful. But I am getting over it fast. I'm almost finished with my hardcover, very heavy *The Accursed*, but I doubt I'll be haulin' Oates again any time soon. Not when I can carry my library with me instead.

The Subway at the Lake

The subway doors open at Columbus Circle and
the air on the platform is suddenly fresh. Trees
from Central Park, the dew of the morning,
the warming heat of August coming up from the damp grass.

And I am back at Indian Lake, at my grandpa's place there,
playing with my cousins.
Sailboats at the dock, the pier stretching out like train tracks
into the blue-gray water around.

Me, terrified of the dull green grasses
that grow just off shore, hidden beneath the surface
of the water.

My dad, teaching me to swim so my face stay'd dry and I
could see where I was going without my glasses.

My mother, cool sipping from a fragile Martini glass
while she sits on a lawn chair, her feet up on a stool.

My grandmother in the house.
Fish caught by grandpa for supper,
Cards and dice played after coffee,
Marshmallows toasted over the fires on the beach.

Fireflies light up the night sky,
ducking in and out of the bushes.
Wet swimsuits hang on the line.
I can taste the icy too-sweet grape Nehi.

Then the double doors shut on the subway train,
and I am heading down to Seventh Avenue now.

I wish I remembered how to play Pinochle.

On NOT Skiing in Utah Today

There's a very compelling commercial for skiing in Park City, Utah on TV. The gist is to identify where you came from so the ad can reinforce how quickly you can get to Utah and start skiing. There are happy skiers from Indiana, from New York, from Minneapolis, and everyone in the ad who started their day in one place is now happily skiing in Utah. The tag is "Where were you this morning?"

I was in the Bronx.

And I didn't go to Park City, Utah for the following reasons:

1. I don't ski. I went to a ski lodge in Colorado once and sat by the fireplace sipping hot chocolate all day while my friends were out on the slopes. It was a colossal bore.
2. I had the day off and I figured everyone else would travel on a day off so I never considered leaving town.
3. I spent the day volunteering with the All Stars Project in Manhattan. They do good - I wanted to help them.
4. As beautiful as Utah seems from these ads, I think if I wanted the mountains and the breathtaking views, since I am not a skier, I might probably go to Montana. I looked into that once. Or Spain.
5. There's a real serious snowstorm on its way east and, with my luck, I'd get to Utah and not be able to get back to the Bronx.

But here's the bigger question: when you consider where you were this morning, assuming you didn't go to Utah either, did you get anywhere today?

That's my question right now. These days I want to establish where I am in the morning so that by nightfall, I can also establish where I have been. Not the simple geography of the route I traveled, but the more substantive stuff. I need to know I got someplace.

So the answer today is yes, I started out in the Bronx,

and yes, I ended up in the Bronx, but I greeted some very nice people today at my volunteer job and I really felt like I contributed something to my fellow New Yorkers. We are a really hearty bunch, all in all, but there are lots of folks who need something I might be able to offer them.

I don't feel sad that I spent the day NOT skiing in Utah today. Utah can wait. And hey, you never know, I just might try skiing. Some days you end up where you start out but, in fact, you are really just a little farther ahead.

Today was one of those days.

The Mists of a Royal Past in Paris

In 2007, I took my daughter, my friend, and my cousin on a weeklong trip to Paris. We rented an atelier in the 6th, we shopped, we ate, we toured museums, and we even bought tickets on a *bateau mouche* for a nighttime tour of the Seine to see all the important monuments lit up. I had a fabulous time because I adore Paris in a way I have never felt about a place where I lived. I cherish my home town in Michigan, I delight in Chicago, I feel comfortable living in New York, and I am constantly challenged by Madrid, but I adore Paris. It holds my heart.

It was on this trip in 2007 that I finally fell in love with what is arguably the heart of Paris: the Cathedral of Notre Dame. In one of my Columbia University art history seminars, we studied medieval Paris and how this huge building went up. I learned how it replaced earlier churches, how it influenced other buildings, and how it helped to establish "Gothic." I read Victor Hugo and learned how he felt about the atrocities of the French Revolution mobs that decapitated the sculpted figures of the biblical kings that spread out along the façade, thinking they were depicting the French aristocracy.

But through all this study, learning about all this conflict and chaos, I could not find my way around this building so that it would start to feel like anything but a bus station. To me, it was a tourist trap of the worst kind. I resented standing in line to get in, I hated the way nobody looked up at these wounded and restored sculptures on their way in, and I thought the machines that spat out gold coins with the image of the church were crass and out of place in what should have been a more solemn house of worship.

This particular trip in 2007 was a photo tour, though. I had a new point-and-shoot camera and I pointed and shot everything that came into my view finder. I thought maybe if I could focus on detail and not the whole experience of Notre Dame, I might find the essence of history that I was missing. So I sat down in front of the building, on one of those stone slabs about 100 feet from the front doors, and I started taking pictures. I zoomed in on faces and objects in a way I hadn't before, figuring, in the worst case scenario, I might get a nice screensaver out of it. I walked up to the façade and took close ups of the doorways and the small stone sculptures that were so important to the first visitors in the year 1250 and are nearly incomprehensible to most tourists now. And even though I know that most of this sculpted façade dates from the mid-19th century renovation and not the 13th century, I started to make the connection.

Our trip was nearly over when my daughter told me she would volunteer to get up just before dawn with me so I could take pictures of Notre Dame before daylight, when maybe all the tourists would still be in bed. I was really touched. We set an alarm, hailed a cab, and found ourselves standing on the opposite side of the plaza in the dark and, once the cab left, we were completely alone. There were no tourists or school groups. There were no hordes of confused-looking "If this is Tuesday, this must be Paris" bus people. It was just us and the sky was not yet ready for daylight.

We made our way across the empty plaza where we found a middle-aged man in a porter's uniform, smoking a cigarette just outside the door on the right where most people enter Notre Dame when it is open. We walked up to him and started to make some small talk about the weather and how different everything looked at this hour compared to later in the day. We were just two American tourists and this was his break in the routine that would prepare the Cathedral for the first Mass at 7:00 a.m.

And then he asked us in.

We smiled and he just opened the door and we walked inside. Unlike any other time of day, the Cathedral was empty; cavernous and empty. All the way up the center aisle, there was someone carpet-sweeping the floor around the altar. The lights over the altar were lit, but the rest of the nave was dark. And it was in that instant that a thousand years of history came swirling around us. I felt the thrill of King Louis IX as he approached the altar in 1249, walking barefoot, carrying his latest treasure: the Crown of Thorns. I felt the arrogance of Napoleon in 1804, surrounded by minions and sycophants, as he snatched the emperor's crown for himself. I suddenly understood why Hugo wanted so desperately to defend this church and why Viollet-le-Duc took such care in saving it. Even though the room was silent, I could hear Gregorian Chant hanging softly in the air above the heads of countless medieval pilgrims.

We walked out into the clear morning air and the porter took our picture sitting in two empty sculpture niches outside. We looked like two American tourists on our way back to the bus, but, in fact, we were two New Yorkers, too stunned to speak, wanting to savor the moment we had spent in this Cathedral all by ourselves, lost in the crowd of history.

We were only inside for a few minutes. It never even occurred to me to take out my camera.

The Perfect Peach

I'm a huge fan of summer fruit. I grew up in an area of Michigan that my mother always called the Fruit Belt. I'm not sure it is really, but it was license enough to me to revel in all the wonderful fresh fruits I could get my hands on during the summer as a kid.

Sometimes, local farmers would drive up and down the streets in the neighborhood offering freshly picked strawberries, or peaches, and vegetables off the back of their trucks. There were a couple of regular guys who'd drive by with their kids. They'd pull over and my mother would bring them a few quarters and then carry everything back up to the house in her apron.

And sometimes, I would go out picking fruit with my dad. We'd get baskets and go out into the fields to select our own strawberries. I loved that. The warm, dry dirt of the fields, the narrow and neat rows with the colorful fruit set against the dark green leaves, and the idea that I was selecting only the most perfect berries to bring home to my mother for shortcake. I loved shortcake and my mother made it without any added sugar so the flavor of the berries was all you got, drizzled and layered over hot fresh, split biscuits.

As I write this, it's late July and if you drive around the county right now, you will be flanked on both sides of most roads by orchards filled with fruit hanging from the trees, so many you can't count them all. The apples are getting close to ripe now and they will take over from the summer fruit before long.

But now, there's peaches. There's something mystical about peaches, something wonderful that I can't give over to other fruit, even the ones that I love, like apples or melons or grapes. There's the tang in the scent of a ripe peach, the overwhelmingly sugary taste, and that uniquely fuzzy feel of the skin as you turn it over in your hands that makes a peach unlike anything else, at least in this part of the country. I tell people who aren't from around here, if you can't smell the peaches from the car, it's not worth getting out to buy the fruit. And nectarines, to me, pale by comparison. I have to have the fuzz.

I was in the county where I grew up just last weekend for a short visit. And I told my dad, all I wanted was a perfect peach. He laughed at me and said most of the peaches were already done, but I persevered and found two spots to try them. We pulled over to one farm stand and found fresh peaches by the bushel for sale with the farmer waiting for us at a service table, holding a rosy peach in his hand to offer us a taste. The peach was so ripe you could peel the skin off with your hands and the pit came right out of the center.

Suddenly it was like Proust with his Madeleines. I tasted the peach and memories of walking through orchards, picking peaches with my dad came back and enriched the flavor in my mouth. I was nine years old again and my dad was calling me to get back in the car before we were late for supper. The car would fill with the thick scent of fresh-picked treasure and I would sleep all the way home, smiling at my good fortune.

I brought a paper bag of peaches back to New York that survived one rental car, three airports, two planes, and a car service ride home. They're gone now, shared with my daughter, all except one lone peach that sits in my kitchen, waiting for me to finish it, to end the adventure.

On the one hand, I should eat it now before it goes bad, because of all fruit, peaches are indeed among the most fragile. But on the other hand, some protocol or ceremony to eating it is in order. I should take pictures or use my glass plate.

It is, after all, a perfect peach.

Dream Weaving and Home

There's an exercise you can do when you feel confused or lost or indecisive. You imagine the place where you feel confident, located, clear. You just close your eyes, breathe calmly, and let the image of that clear, wonderful place come to mind. It's the place where you are happy, the place where you feel calm. This is the place where you believe you are meant to be, your center.

I wonder why it is that the place I imagine is never "home."

I picture beaches and sun when it rains or lovely gardens with cool breezes when it's hot, but I never imagine being home. I see myself getting on a plane or passing through turnstiles on my way to board a train, strangers moving quickly ahead of me. I see myself sitting in front of a Gothic cathedral, sipping coffee, gazing at the façade and watching pilgrims come and go, most of them not even looking up.

Sometimes, I do this on a crowded bus, just to see what is the first thing that comes to mind. I'm on the edge of a pier, looking out over the water to sailboats glistening in the distance. Or I'm in a library, surrounded by books and silence. When I come around, I'm still on the bus, but now I am curious that if I am in fact, in that moment, on my way home, why is it I am not projecting toward the moment I open the door? Wouldn't that be the one object of desire on that bus?

I have a lovely home, filled with people I love, people who love me, and if I complained even once, I would surely go straight to Hell. But there is an interesting disconnect between my path home and my imaginary place of calm, of peace, of stillness and happiness.

Most of it has to do with daydreams being about places I don't know or haven't seen, like India. I don't know many beaches so when I imagine the hammock and the umbrella drinks, it's from ads for beach vacations, not experience. There are times when I imagine being completely happy in Paris or Madrid, two cities I know fairly well. I'd be at one of my favorite haunts with time on my hands and cash in my backpack. I could be hiking through fields and forests and farms. I just don't dream of going home, not to my parents' house where I grew up, not to the first apartment I had when I got married, and not to the place I live now.

I can't give up the exercise because it is so revealing. But I think I might start taking notes to see if I can find a pattern – do I center on more beaches than towns, more hiking than sitting?

Unlike a lot of people, if I really can't find my center, I can always move. It's the cheater's way out, but I might just do that. Spain is nice.

Aunt Em had just come out of the house to water the cabbages when she looked up and saw Dorothy running toward her.

"My darling child!" she cried, folding the little girl in her arms and covering her face with kisses. "Where in the world did you come from?"

"From the Land of Oz," said Dorothy gravely. "And here is Toto, too. And oh, Aunt Em! I'm so glad to be at home again!"

L. Frank Baum, *The Wonderful Wizard of Oz*

Glazed Doughnuts and Church

Since I have not lived in my home town for over 40 years, I have also not been a recent member of my home church, but last week I went back for a few days to visit my family. On Sunday, I sat quietly and looked around, trying to recall what I would have seen in that exact place when I was in school.

They've moved the choir downstairs from the choir loft and painted the inside of the church more than a few times, but most of it looks about the same to me. I could almost hear the jangling of the rosaries and crosses that hung from the nuns' religious habits as they walked up and down the aisles, making sure we behaved ourselves.

Then I looked around at the faces of the folks near me on Sunday, looking for anyone I went to school with, but I couldn't find any of those children there. The only faces I saw there were of gray-haired, tired people I didn't recognize. On the one hand, they looked familiar, but on the other, I couldn't say for sure they were anyone I ever knew.

As I sat there on Sunday, I looked for the boy in Grade 5 who I was sure I wanted to marry. I wanted to see the boy who kissed me on my front stoop in Grade 7. Or any of the children I remember now from the few black and white photographs I have that were taken on school picture days. But these were children's faces I was looking for and the children I went to school with are now all grown and in their 60s.

I'm not sure what happened to all of them after I left town, just four years after Eighth Grade graduation. I heard some time ago that one joined the Coast Guard, I know another married the local track star I dated in high school, and a girl had married the mayor's son. He's buried now with his father near my mother's grave in the church cemetery.

How could I think I could find, in the faces of these sixty-something senior citizens, the children I played with in school, the ones who dressed in red caps and white gowns for

Confirmation or puffy white dresses for May pageants? There I was, looking for still black and white images of children in a murky sea of gray, real, grown-up life. All of those children are gone now, lost to time. They were replaced by gray-haired, tired people whose own children are now grown and I just didn't know them.

In Grade 2, after we had made our First Communion, the nuns at my school had to devise a way to feed the entire class breakfast inside the classroom after daily Mass because, at that time, Catholics were not allowed to eat anything for three hours before taking the Host. It was later reduced to one hour without eating, which was still not entirely practical when you are trying to get small kids out to school and daily Mass starts at 8:00 a.m. every day.

So, after Mass, as we started at school, the nuns would have their classrooms filled with blessed, but starving, children. To resolve this, in one of my most pleasant memories, the local doughnut baker would arrive in our classroom with freshly made glazed doughnuts on a wheeled cart that held tiny containers of white and chocolate milk. The doughnuts cost a nickel, I think; milk was two or three cents. After eating, we would start our lessons.

You know, I still like glazed doughnuts. And every time I have one, I remember the cart the baker brought, with the white and chocolate milk, and the noise of hungry, clamoring children, lining up for breakfast, fresh from Mass and ready to start the day. They were my friends then.

The bakery has gone out of business and I am a gray-haired, tired person myself now. I prefer black coffee with my doughnuts and I don't eat them all that often, but I am always open to change.

Finding the Us in Fried Chicken

When I was little, we used to go to my mother's family on Sundays. Most days, we'd have roast beef with my grandfather's famous mashed potatoes. But sometimes, when nobody wanted to cook or we had cousins coming over, we'd go to Colonel Sanders for a bucket of fried chicken and it was like we had just picked up a party. There'd be biscuits and paper plates and we'd joke about how the individual pieces didn't resemble any chicken parts we were familiar with.

Not one member of my family ever made fried chicken, not once, not ever. You'd think since everyone liked it, someone would make it. But it remained the one thing we bought from strangers that we never prepared for ourselves. We made our own hamburgers, even though we went to McDonald's, we made our own pizza, even though we phoned in a pie every so often, and we made our own pasta dishes, all the while loving Italian restaurants. But for some reason, fried chicken was the elusive, the other, the thing we had to buy that we couldn't produce for ourselves.

So you can imagine my unbridled joy when I found a world-class fried chicken place in our new neighborhood when we moved to the Bronx. It is called US Chicken, which I imagine, given the red, white, and blue awning, is meant to be U.S. for "United States Chicken." I call it "Us Chicken" and it quickly became a weekly staple in my house. It was like we were "us."

And then, suddenly and without warning, they closed. I was heartbroken, cast adrift, confused. Like losing any great habit, I couldn't figure out what to do next. I tried going to Kentucky Fried Chicken but it was crowded, the counter help was not helpful, and it was way more expensive than my regular "Us" order.

I started asking around the neighborhood and heard it was the Board of Health that had closed up the place, that they had "issues." I didn't want to believe it. I felt protective and I trusted Us to run a clean shop. But everyone I spoke with said the same thing, so I decided to get closer to the source and I asked the corner banana man if he knew anything. He told me they had closed to renovate the place and put in pizza ovens. Banana Guy had spoken to somebody who knew somebody and he reassured me they would reopen soon.

It was only about two weeks later that I saw some signs of life. Us was cleaning and opening boxes of new equipment and hanging new signs. Not only do they have pizza now, they have little tables so it's not just take-out. My favorite chicken guy didn't come back, but my favorite chicken is right where I want it and the new counter guy is really nice.

As much as I could have gotten used to Kentucky Fried Chicken, I really did feel like Us was us. It is my local place, it is part of my neighborhood, and the people who work there matter. I am so happy they added pizza to the menu because that delivery business will cover them for quite a while. I tried the new onion rings and they give you free biscuits now.

And hey, it's not like I'm going to start making my own fried chicken any time soon. We just don't do that in my family.

Remembering Camelot

It's remarkable how fresh your personal memories can be when they are part of a collective national tragedy. What I recall and what I can speak about today is just my tiny needle sitting atop the haystack of newspaper and magazine articles that were printed in 1963 and the dozens if not hundreds of newscasts, radio broadcasts, and a handful of TV and Hollywood movies - everyone telling what they remembered in the way they remembered it.

I remember *Camelot.*

I was 8 years old when John Fitzgerald Kennedy won the presidential election in 1960. My family fell on both sides of the aisle in those days with my grandfather working in politics in Chicago and everyone else in ongoing debate about the fact that Kennedy was first, Irish, and then, Catholic. He was us. And as many historians will tell you today, among those who were fortunate enough to have known him in those few years of his presidency, there was something special about him.

Kennedy won in November and the next month, on December 3, 1960, the enchanting Lerner and Loew musical, *Camelot*, opened on Broadway and from that moment, what I remember was that the two events were suddenly running simultaneously in the national consciousness and in my childhood. Kennedy was the designated heir apparent to the Massachusetts Kennedy family legacy in politics and King Arthur, in the musical on Broadway, was his mythical counterpart.

It was a classic case of our wanting something we couldn't have - royalty - and substituting a fiction we could live with - a perfectly beautiful, perfectly wonderful, perfectly lovely family with a smart, well-educated, engaging father, a stunningly beautiful and unbelievably photogenic wife and mother, with two perfectly adorable children, surrounded by endless possibility and even more endless wealth. We all knew we could never be them, but we were all glad that at the very least, we could watch them.

And in the end, the shocking death, the heartbreaking funeral, and that eternal flame burning at Arlington just fit together to form my memory of JFK. He appeared, he enchanted us, and he died in a terrible, terrible way. And we can fill in the blanks of his life now - or not.

We can now just remember *Camelot.*

Did he have affairs, was he indecisive on key international politics, was there anything glossed over, or fudged about his military background? It doesn't matter. It didn't matter then either. We had built a beautiful fantasy and we were all living in it together.

When he died, and everyone said "they" had killed him, I fully expected to see a group of men, rounded up, on the evening news that night. And then it turned out to be that one man. That one, small, non-descript man, who for an unknown reason had taken aim at some considerable distance and shot dead the president we all loved unconditionally. It was as if the floor had dropped out from under us and we just kept falling with the music of Lerner and Loew playing in the background.

When it was all over, we went slowly back to the lives we had lived before 1960. The only problem was we had seen, for those few years, a glimpse of something so delectable, so magical, that I think now, it's that specific loss of innocence that I remember most. We were forced to grow up very quickly and to see that even the Broadway musical that ran underneath our fantasy was something finite. Lovely, but finite.

It's true! It's true!
The crown has made it clear.
The climate must be perfect all the year.
A law was made a distant moon ago here:
July and August cannot be too hot.
And there's a legal limit to the snow here
In Camelot.

The winter is forbidden till December
And exits March the second on the dot.
By order, summer lingers through September
In Camelot.

I remember Jack Kennedy.
It's how that summer lingers through September.

I'm Not Busy

My mother always said, if you want to get out of a social engagement, just say you are busy. It wasn't really lying and that was sufficient. You could be busy and that was not only an acceptable counter activity, it was acceptable period. It was OK to be busy.

I was able to carry on with this delusion for quite a while. When I was in college, I worked at a local precursor to Walmart called Lou Ann's. I sold guns and toys and when the store was quiet, I was told to look busy. I would take a rag from under the counter and I would go out into the department and put the toys back together and sort and organize the bullets and pellets. I came to realize that being busy actually meant you had nothing to do.

Now I was worried. What if all the people I had told I was busy found out what I found out, that being busy meant you had nothing to do? That made me nervous, so I started telling people I couldn't meet them after work because I had to "get home." I wasn't sure what that meant, but it seemed to work more often than not, so that replaced "I´m busy."

Then I wondered, why did my mother not want to socialize with anyone, why was she always "busy?" I am still not sure of the real answer to that one, but when I left Lou Ann's and started to meet people and get more social invitations, I found that either I had to go or I would have to come up with better excuses. "Get home" didn't work so well when I was living alone because I never had animals to let out or feed, and "I'm busy" had completely lost its charm.

So I started accepting invitations to go to dinner, to go get drinks, to sit and converse with other people instead of staying in my house by myself. Now I had friends, I knew restaurants, I could talk about the newspapers and CNN. I was with it. Not only was I out there, but I had interests and I could make small talk with the best of them.

The thing about being a social person was that I found I didn't want to say I was "busy" or had to "get home" because I started enjoying people, asking questions, having people ask me questions. Hell, I was communicating and I liked that! I liked it lots.

Later in my mother's life, I found she just stopped going out altogether. She didn't go to bookstores, which I know she enjoyed. She stopped going to music club events or meetings of the Altar and Rosary Society. I am not sure which stopped first, but the end result was she became really good at being busy to the point where she went nowhere at all. She was the same kind of busy I was at Lou Ann's, when there was nothing to do.

I think it is tempting to be busy. You don't have to meet anyone's expectations; you are never too early or late for an appointment. You can't be wearing the wrong shoes. Everyone just thinks you're busy.

But I think there's a tipping point to this. I think there's a moment where the people you know stop asking where you are, stop looking for you in the crowded place as they compare notes and look at their watches. I think there's a moment only you know you've reached where they just stop thinking of you and you slip out of notice completely.

You know, I thought that's what had happened to my mother, but when she died, people came from everywhere to tell me how her language ability specifically was what they remembered about her. The way she read books to them when they were small, or how well she spoke, or the way she wrote letters, or enjoyed a good joke, these were the things these people thought of when they remembered her.

So, I'm not busy.

I will be there.

Let me get my coat.

Manhattan Morning in August

Hill blocks view.
The sign says: Hill blocks view.

So what don't you see?
What's just out of view?
What's blocked before you take the hill?

Just the local electronics store, gates still down.
Graffiti on the wall over the market.

The long truck, making deliveries at the grocery store
With all those boxes to open.

The telephone store, the new phone is *protegida en la playa*
And the mini mart man is uncrating the fruit.

There's a tall shampoo girl
Washing an early patron at Fantasy Hair,
And a man in a yellow shirt, sitting alone on a street bench,
Looking at his hands.

Three men with their paper cup coffees are
Shooting what little breeze they can find.

A rasher of day lilies, bursting red orange,
Leaning out to the street,
An American flag is stuck on a post against the wall that
hides the subway.

The dad taking two girls to day camp
Them, clutching his hand, and
Him, clutching a small stuffed giraffe.

A man dressed all in white, wearing a turban,

Organizing, sorting the stack of free papers next to the stairs.
The prayer book women with the demure long skirts
Holding their holy tracts,
The ambulance screaming at them,
Setting all those gray birds to flight.

It's too early for the dominoes games
But they'll be here later,
Upended milk crates for seats around a folding table.
The clack of the tiles slapping the board,
Everyone wanting to get in on the action.

One lone woman walks across the street dressed all in black,
Carrying a lime green umbrella on this impossibly sunny day.

It's a Manhattan blue sky morning
And there's a running thread.
It knits these people,
These places together
All blocked from view,
By a hill.

It's Not the Books, It's the Library

It's easy to identify the Nancy Drew and Dana Girls mysteries as my favorite children's adventure stories. When I read those little books, I wanted to be the one with the answer, the one to solve the crime, the one to show the grown-ups that this teen could do it. These girls were resourceful and clever. What's interesting to me now is that, for the life of me, I cannot recall a single episode and I couldn't name more than one title. I do not remember just exactly what these plucky heroines accomplished. What I do remember is my cousin Diane.

Diane was much older than me. She was a child of the 1940s whose father served in WWII. She spent countless hours with my grandparents and her aunt and uncle, laying a foundation of trust and love for all of the cousins to follow. We all knew that we were important and we knew that our family had something special, and a good bit of that came from the first cousin on the scene: Diane.

I came to know Nancy Drew because Diane collected the books. As far as I can remember, it was a complete set. I could borrow them, read them one at a time or a couple at a go, and return them to her collection. But it was never about the plot of the books, it was that Diane could read and when she did, she did it up in style. I could take books out of the town public library certainly, and I did that nearly every week I was in school. But Diane *had* a library and that was exciting to me.

Because my family did not have a budget line for book buying or the means to get to bookstores very often, and because I spent so much time at the library, I have only a dozen or so books from my childhood. I do not have all the great pirate books that I loved. I don't have the stories of Pompeii that I remember so clearly. And I don't have the Nancy Drew books. I vowed that when I had my own children, I would buy them books instead of just taking them to the library. I wanted them to know what Diane must have known, that there is tremendous comfort in being in a library, but there is something so much more powerful in owning a library.

Diane left us a few years ago. She had a heart ailment that would take her from us way too soon. In writing this, I am sad she doesn't know the lifelong impact her choice in teen fiction had on me. I want her to know that her collecting Nancy Drew and Dana Girl mysteries, and sharing them the way she did, instilled in me a love of libraries as well as a love of a great mystery story. My library has books about everything!

I'm reading my own copy of *The Daughter of Time* by Josephine Tey now with my book club and even though it does not feature crimes to solve, a boyfriend with a slick convertible, or helpful aunts and uncles, it does remind me of the debt I owe to my cousin Diane.

It's great to have a library card, but it's even better to have a library.

Just a Book Signing at Books of Wonder

It was my son's Grade 3 teacher who introduced us all to Harry Potter. She was from the UK and she discovered the first book and read it in bits to the class and then sent it home with the kids so they could finish it. I took over reading it to my kids every night but we only got about a chapter and a half in before I found myself staying up late and getting up early just to read about Harry.

This was a challenging time in my house and reading together was very important to us. We all became fans, we bought the first, then the second book. And when the third book came out, I read that J.K. Rowling herself was scheduled to appear at a local children's bookstore and I took the afternoon off from work and went over to stand in line just to be able to get signed copies and meet the woman who created Hogwarts.

When I got to the line, I was giddy. I rehearsed what I was going to say, over and over again, because I knew from experience that I would likely only have about 23 seconds to say or do anything - roughly the time it would take for her to open her book, sign, slide the book over, smile.

I bought the first two books again and she signed all three for me. And as she was signing, I told her that my whole family wanted her to know that we wished her to be very rich and very happy. She replied, "I am very happy - and I am getting very rich." I was thrilled.

The glorious footnote to this small exchange is that Books of Wonder was one of the very first places in the U.S. to recognize how extraordinary that first book was. They contracted her for a signing shortly after it was published here but because they worried such an unknown author wouldn't draw flies, they had her appear with another writer. She was the proverbial opening act.

Every so often I price signed first editions of J.K. Rowling's books but there is no way I could sell them. They are the symbol of splendid writing, marvelous, captivating storytelling, and a time in my children's lives when we all needed a little escape and Harry Potter filled the bill.

Here's to you, J.K.! And the wonderful wizarding world you created for us.

Little Notes under the Door

Written communication has come a long way, you might say, from the quill and the ink stand, the parchment and the wax seal. But even though we spend way more time typing our thoughts on a keyboard, little notes still get through. Sometimes they are posted with stamps, the way people did in the last century, and sometimes, you get a note under the door.

I live in a typical New York apartment building. It's Pre-War - which means built before the outbreak of the Second World War - and it's got a particularly nice vibe. There is a strong community here with multi-generational families on many floors and a sense that the building matters and the people who live here care not only about the building but about each other.

So, sometimes, you get a note under your door. Last night, it was personalized by being addressed to my apartment number. Not to me personally by my name, but to me, the apartment number. That's fine - to be fair, we are new-ish to the building and most people don't know my name. The note said that the porter's mother had died and that the other tenants had gotten her a Mass card and did I want to sign it.

There's almost no other way this could have been communicated to me. I don't share my E-mail address with other tenants, and I leave so early in the morning that I just about never run into people. When I come into the building in the evening, I go right home and lock up for the night. That's not a bad thing necessarily, but it does preclude information-sharing by face to face.

So, there's the note under the door. At the end of the note, there was a request that if I did want to contribute a little something to a gift or sign the Mass card, I could, by leaving a note under the door of the unnamed tenant who left that note under my door.

And so it goes.

One note to my apartment, requesting a kindness for a worker in the building. Then the chain follows down the hall when I leave "a little something" in another note, left under the door. I don't know the tenant in the apartment who left the first note for me, but maybe I'll knock and sign the card. It would be a chance for me to meet someone. Someone who was kind enough to slip that note under my door so I knew about the mother's death.

Nobody was home when I knocked on the door. I ran into the porter this morning on my way out. I gave her my condolences.

Saving Grace

When I had my first child, I didn't know very much about children and unlike lots of first time moms, I didn't have any family around me to fill in the blanks. I took everything at face value and proceeded like I knew what I was doing, hoping everything would be just fine. In fact, I did, like a lot of first time moms, lots of dumb things. I assumed, for instance that everyone I know would be sitting by their mailboxes waiting for the photo of the month I sent out to them. Each month, I would prop up the kid, take dozens of photos, and send them out to the Club. What was I thinking?

The Kid was pretty cool, all in all, and a great companion to me. I took her everywhere to the point where the New York Times sent out a photographer and a writer to cover my story. Doesn't everyone bring The Kid to dress rehearsals of the Philharmonic, trending Upper East Side bruncheries, or the Metropolitan Museum of Art? I wasn't going to stop going there myself just because I had The Kid, so she came along with me. And then, when she was about 18 months old, she started teaching herself to read by sounding out the letters on ads in store windows. And I was very proud. Since I knew nothing about children, I thought everyone did that at 18 months.

When I started to look at pre-schools, I decided I would just let The Kid do her thing in the interviews and I would see how she stacked up to the other kids. This was the first time she would be exposed to other children on any consistent basis and the experience was eye-opening. We went to interview at a Montessori school that I'd heard about. It was a bright, colorful place but I found the artwork disturbing. It wasn't that the images were of disturbing things, but that every single, last picture was completely and entirely identical to the next except they were signed by different children. The Kid sat down to replicate the prototype and missed a key element. She was told to draw a snowman just like the model but she didn't include the blue scarf, so the teacher prompted her by asking if she'd forgotten something in the drawing. The Kid looked at her and said, "Eyebrows?" And then she didn't get in.

We went to a standard private school she liked and she was accepted immediately. She loved the classroom, the children, the teachers, and the routine. At first. Her drawings were simple at first, then more complex, adding trees, sun, clouds, more people, more houses. There was an obvious progression from simple to complex and I thought everything was fine until I went for the parent meeting and they told me about The Kid and the puzzle she had solved that morning. It was the most complicated puzzle in the classroom and The Kid had completed it in just a few minutes, something they had never seen before. I thought, that's great, but what does she do tomorrow? They told me, she could re-solve the same puzzle again and again because that was all they had for her. I realized their modus operandi was simply to pull everyone to the center, by bringing up the slower students and slowing down the really capable ones. We started looking for another school.

Kindergarten interviews are a little different from preschool ones because they rely more on social interaction. The Kid was tested for a small gifted program at a New York City public school and she scored in the top three percentile and was accepted. I was apprehensive about sending The Kid to a public school because I had never attended a public school myself and had no idea what to do first. But like my other parenting efforts, I decided to take an active role so I volunteered to write and edit the program's newsletter. I could keep an eye on The Kid and the school at the same time. I expected the worst and found the best, the best approach to learning, the best teachers, the best kids, and the perfect place for The Kid.

The Kid's first teacher was a woman I will call Miss Case. She was serious, friendly, interesting, and, as it turned out, God's very gift to teachers. She had an extreme math ability that suited her precocious charges and she sent home homework none of the parents could do. I remember calling around the phone tree trying to find anyone older than five who could master the mathematical concepts Miss Case was teaching. She took them on school trips to museums so they could see patterns and shapes they would discuss back at school. The children in this classroom couldn't wait to get there in the morning and they didn't want to leave in the afternoon.

The only thing better than having Miss Case in Kindergarten was when the parents found out she was being reassigned to Grade 5 just as our children were about enter the Grade 5. These gifted kids had been given their own gift. They had been given the chance to reconnect with Miss Case and they were thrilled. She took the extraordinary concepts she had taught them five years earlier and spun them into even more intricate patterns and shapes that they could take on to Middle School, high school, and college.

The Kid became a civil engineer and in so many ways, I thank this one New York City public school teacher. Miss Case was underpaid certainly but worth her weight in gold to The Kid. If we had stayed at that lovely private school, The Kid never would have felt that her crazy math ability was in any way normal and even kind of cool. In the public school gifted program, she was surrounded by children who challenged her and teachers who could keep her busy and working.

Right now, if you asked me to pay more taxes for the benefit of the teacher my daughter had in 1991, I would do so with tears in my eyes, tears of gratitude for the teacher who saved my kid. So much is written and argued about the kids in the lowest percentile, but rarely do the writers understand what it is to have a gifted child in that top percentile. This public school was a life raft to the two of us.

My standard explanation to people who think gifted programs cater to the elite is this: it's like giving two children the task of washing the dishes. The smart child will use hot water, plenty of soapy suds, they will scrub the Dickens out of each dish, dry them completely, and put them away in neat rows. The gifted kid will find a way to get the smart kid to do it for them.

I am still proud of my kid. She solves the Rubik's cube in under a minute. And she's happy.

It Was the Nuns

I've never really taken to the word "mentor." It's not a word that was really popular when I was in school so I never sought out someone to take that role. It's not that I didn't have wonderful role models and teachers throughout my academic career and it's not that I thought I didn't need someone to give me personal guidance. I just never knew it was an option.

Looking back though, I realize now that it was the nuns I had in school who made the biggest impact on my life. My parents were there every step of the way, supportive and loving, but it was a handful of really important religious women who gave me the real life skills I use every day. They were the dedicated nuns who taught me in school.

Grade 1 - My first grade teacher taught me to read and when I got really good at it, she would pull books out of the Grade 3 library for me to take home after the other kids left for the day.

Grade 2 - My second grade teacher told my parents I couldn't see the kid in front of me, let alone the blackboard. I still remember the day I finally got my first pair of glasses and could see the flames on the candles on the altar at church. That was a day.

Grade 5 - Diagramming sentences and conjugating verbs. Words fail me when I try to describe the value of those skills.

Grade 6 - I skipped a grade so I didn't actually go to Grade 6, but the Mother Superior taught me how to fry eggs over the summer between Grades 5 and 7. I liked that a lot.

Grade 7 - My seventh grade teacher let me think I was a secret agent. She taught my class in Grade 8 too and even pretended to be a spy on special assignment. In some crazy way, she gave validation to my desire to travel and learn languages.

High School - I had the most amazing teacher of my life in high school. She taught French in the most creative ways. On our first day in her class, she wrote symbols on the blackboard instead of letters. I know now it was phonetic spellings of the words, but she said we were to ignore what we knew about language and just trust her that we would learn to speak French and enjoy it. By the time I was a junior, I was fluent. I thought everyone who took high school French could carry on long, elaborate, idiom-filled conversations in French. We went to Mass in French, we saw French films on the weekends, and attended performances of French theater. It was just what we did.

Then, she disappeared. One day she was teaching us French, the next day she was gone and she was replaced in the classroom with a woman who spoke Canadian French none of us could understand. It turned out, this gifted French teacher had quietly learned to speak Spanish, and if I am remembering this episode correctly, she just quit her religious order, and moved to Miami to teach English to Cuban refugees who were arriving there every day. It was the last we heard about her. She had immersed herself in Spanish and given up her career in order to help people. The order wanted her to teach spoiled private girls' school French, but she knew her real calling was to help Cuban refugees.

Was she my real mentor? This whole incident knocked me out. I was stunned and proud and fascinated all at once, but what has stayed with me all these years was her commitment to what she knew she was supposed to do. She knew her skills in French would stand her in good stead in any language and that she could use those skills in a new way to make the lives of her new students just a little bit better.

Mentors come and go and, in many business situations, you can hitch your little wagon to the wrong guy. They can take you along until your fresh ideas no longer amuse them or they can just give you all the work and take all the credit. Mentees don't get a lot of respect. But a great teacher can change your life. This one French teacher was my mentor. She taught me so much more than French that I could almost forget just how much I learned sitting in her class. When I arrived in Paris for the first time 14 years after she left for Miami, I had dinner with two non-English speakers. I hadn't used my French in years but after just about 20 minutes, it all came back to me and I spent the evening discussing politics and music and the weather.

But it was what happened when we left the restaurant that really reminded me of her. I was able to recognize a few key buildings and find my way to the apartment without a map because my French book had the map of Paris inside the cover and she made us memorize it.

Never take teachers for granted. You don't always know everything they've taught you while you are still in their classroom. Sometimes, you know by looking back.

Out of the Melting Pot

Lots of families can claim at least one family historian. Having collected piles of data, they surface at family gatherings, weaving a tapestry of slender genetic threads through generations of relations. And then they bore everyone to extinction, remarkably, with their findings. They collect photos, newspaper articles, cemetery rubbings, maps, census sheets, and church records. How do I know all this? That's what I do. And let me tell you, nothing thrills me more than a chance to visit a fresh cemetery.

If you watch the Lifetime show sponsored by Ancestry Dot Com, *Who Do You Think You Are*, you can get an idea of the type of genealogical work that goes into building a family tree. You start with someone in the family who either has information or needs information and you build from whatever you have. In my case, when I started I knew next to nothing about my family. I knew that my father's family "came over on the boat with the Studebakers." And I knew my mother's family was almost exclusively Irish, with the exception of one colorful lady who, according to family legend, was "a lady of the Spanish court."

With only those little bits, a couple of names, and access to a university library system, I set out to find out who I thought I was. I plugged names into databases, including a particularly good one at the Mormon Church, and I started printing out pages of information and jotting down scores of names, dates, and places. And I was confident it would take me only a short while to get the tree back to the pioneers; to the people who were the first to come to the U.S. from someplace else.

Well, years later, I am perhaps the most boring individual on this planet. I have over 600 names in the family tree, I can tell you stories about soldiers, asylums, and siblings till the cows come home, and I probably know who owned the cows. I have information on dozens of surnames, many countries, rival political agendas, and innumerable marriages, baptisms, and deaths. I've taken trips to cemeteries and churches, looking for the trace of my ancestors in other places, like Ireland and France. It's been a tremendous success, even though, in the process, I have bored nearly as many people as are currently in the family tree.

So I doubt seriously that my father's family came to this country with any of the Studebakers. That was interesting to me, that they would veil the truth about their journey here to latch onto this famous family. I have yet to find the Spanish lady either, but I will keep looking for her because she intrigues me.

What I do know is this: based on this research and with some authority, I can now become anyone I like. That's been the most fun of all.

On national holidays, I can be the one whose family sold some property to Thomas Jefferson and George Washington so they could build the White House. On military holidays, I can be the direct descendant of someone who fought in the American Revolution at the Battle of White Plains, someone who enlisted in the 47th Indiana Volunteer Infantry to fight for the Union during the Civil War, or someone who was fortunate enough to provide his own horse when he enlisted to fight for the Confederacy with the Shenandoah Rangers in Virginia.

If I want to place my family history in commerce, I can be the great great-granddaughter of the publisher of the Larne Weekly Reporter in Ireland in the 19th century. Or I can be the one whose family owned a succession of blacksmith shops in north central Indiana. I come from several streetcar operators, one soap factory worker, many carpenters, some farmers, and one really fascinating political prisoner who was sold into slavery after the Monmouth Rebellion in 17th century England. I come from car builders, postal workers, house builders, furniture craftsmen, housekeepers, one police officer, and at least three generations of wagon wheel makers. As far as I have been able to discover, and clearly the work continues, we never owned slaves and when many around us were illiterate, we could read and write.

These days, I choose to ally myself with the Spanish lady though. Her name was Isabella. She was someone's mother, I think, although so far, I can't tell whose, and every generation since her time has named a daughter Isabella. Her husband, as the story goes, was an Irish fisherman in my family whose boat was swept off course. He landed in Spain, married her, and brought her back to Ireland. My second daughter carries her name as her middle name. And my modern Isabella is a New York, Madrid, and Seville-trained Spanish dancer.

So, where does this leave me? It leaves me with lots of work to do certainly. After all, Labor Day is coming up and I have this wonderful photograph of my great uncle, standing proudly with the auto workers outside the Studebaker plant in South Bend sometime during the 1930s. For Halloween, I could dress up like my dear uncle who once went as a Killer Bee. I can be whatever I want.

But I want to get my story right even if it's not all that compelling to hear it. It is my story after all.

My Great-Grandmother's Prayer Book

It's hard to say how this little black book came into my hands. It's falling apart and I keep it in a bag these days so the pages won't get lost if they come away from the spine. It's only about 5 1/2 inches tall and it has 689 cream-colored pages of prayers, inspiration, and reflections to accompany the parts of the Catholic Mass. It is almost entirely in English with only a handful of psalms in Latin and it includes a selection of secular writings interspersed with the prayers and Bible passages. It's called simply "My Prayer Book" and it was a gift from my grandmother and my great aunt to their mother, my great-grandmother, on December 25, 1915.

In 1915, my grandmother and her sister were teenagers. They lived on the South Side of Chicago surrounded by family in a thriving Irish community that was at the forefront of Chicago politics. They lived with diseases that are now extinct and life-threatening infections that are now easily cured. These amazing siblings were such a powerful influence to my growing up that I named all of my own children after them.

Even though I never knew my great-grandmother, after reading her prayer book, I liked to think I knew how she prayed. Her prayer book is well worn, the pages are torn in a few places, and the spine is split where she must have used the prayers over and over again. Unlike a lot of prayer books I knew as a child, this particular book is focused on being cheerful, offering small kindnesses to your neighbors, and persevering by concentrating on getting by one day at a time. "Smiling faces make a peaceful, happy home," "A humble man makes merry over his own misadventures," and "Kindness adds sweetness to everything."

There are pages and pages of admonitions to look after the well-being of your neighbors and your children and to remember that a good sense of humor is a tremendous asset. After all, "Humor is the just appreciation of the incongruous things of life."

But it's the prayers for the dead that occupied the reader's time with this book. The pages fall open to two separate sections of prayers to be offered on behalf of those who have died. In the first section, there are a number of days listed after the prayers; indulgences that will benefit the soul of the departed in that exact amount. If you read the prayer on the top of page 289, for example, the soul to which you direct the prayer will spend 100 days fewer in Purgatory for each utterance of the prayer. I remember saying the same small prayer over and over again when I was in grade school in an effort to stack up points against my own inevitable banishment there.

My great-grandmother could have skimmed over the sections asking the reader to remain cheerful. She might not have been all that interested in keeping a sense of humor. She prayed so that her family would be safe and, after she died, my great-grandfather, who survived another twenty years without her, left her funeral card in the back of this book, her prayer book.

My mother wrote me a note years ago saying that it was my great-grandfather who had Scotch-taped a clipping to the card. It's a touching little poem, the kind you see in obituaries in small town newspapers. I think he worried that he wouldn't be able to find her when he reached Heaven.

So the very real possibility is that this sweet little book and these prayers for the dead are his prayers for the repose of *her* soul. I can't begin to understand that level of devotion, that you would spend so many of your prayers on someone else that their eternal suffering might somehow be made less.

Or maybe he prayed for himself, for the repose of his own soul, that his servitude in Limbo be short. That way, he could join her in Heaven that much sooner.

I hope he found her. I hope she knows how much he must have loved her. And I hope they both know the comfort that their great-granddaughter finds every time I open this book. There is some real magic in these pages.

And there is also some real love holding it together.

My House is for Sale

My house is for sale.

No, not the house I live in or the house I own, but the house I covet, the house I long for. I know you aren't supposed to covet your neighbor's wife or your neighbor's house, but I really love this one. It's for sale now and it's breaking my heart that I can't buy it. That's why I call it "my" house.

I have coveted houses of all descriptions for as long as I can remember. At first, it was my school friends' houses. The plan was simple. They would just move away and leave their house to me. Then I could paint or wallpaper, pick out carpets, make sure my dishes and linens matched, move in with my Nancy Drew mysteries and my rainbow-colored xylophone, and live happily ever after. And it's not that I didn't have a lovely home of my own. I have been very fortunate to have lived in wonderful houses and apartments.

In college, I studied the history of houses. I spent a glorious semester once, studying Frank Lloyd Wright houses where, on Saturdays, the entire class drove out to Oak Park, Illinois to see them. We photographed and toured the interiors of over a dozen homes and were able to interview the owners of his houses, too.

Did you know a lot of Wright houses leak? Maybe I should have gone into real estate?

There's something about that one house, the one that stays with you after you walk by. Maybe it's a bigger house when you've outgrown your space, or maybe it's the white picket fence that reminds you of Mark Twain. In my case, it's a house that could have been a rectory. About thirty years ago, if I remember the story correctly, when the church next door to it needed extra funds for a renovation of the church building, the family that owned the house sold it to be able to donate a large amount of money to help out the church. I remember seeing the For Sale signs. It wasn't in fabulous shape then, but it had character. My mother always said a house should have character.

Whoever bought the house then must have had some serious access to extra funds of their own. The grimy exterior brick was cleaned, the weathered window frames were painted a subtle taupe color and, at the time, I felt good, knowing that the place was in good hands. It looked happy. They cleaned up the interior by doing a full historical renovation. I've seen pictures. It's really beautiful. It's a classic 19th century Manhattan townhouse. It has a spectacular staircase and a central stained glass skylight. There are six floors in the floor plan and it has a landscaped back yard.

And now it's for sale again and here I am, standing on the street in front of the house, wishing I could have it. It's fun to imagine what I could do with all that space if they would just move out and leave it to me.

I'd buy a full concert grand piano. I think it would be nice to play the piano after dinner in the evening. I like the idea of having *salons* where singers and players could come to perform together on Sunday afternoons and poets could read their work. The living room is big enough to have a string quartet next to my piano. We could set up some chairs and comfortable couches and serve cookies. There are a couple of assisted living places in this neighborhood where my players could perform too. I could lend everyone space to practice. Voice teachers could come to my house to give lessons and the house would fill with live music.

And there'd be cooking so the house would smell like home. This house has such a huge kitchen I could invite food people in to teach new mothers in the city how to make their own baby food. And we could have cooking classes for children so they could learn how to run a safe kitchen.

Or maybe I could turn over the garden level of my house to an art gallery where artists could show their pictures and sculptures. We could have openings and press events so they could sell their work and I would invite my friends in to preview the shows and snatch up their best pieces. And I will keep some sculptures out in the garden so I can see them while I drink my coffee in the morning.

I could plant string beans. String beans would be nice in the garden. I could cook them with bacon bits like my mother used to cook when I was little. And in the fall, we could put carved pumpkins out on the stoop so the neighborhood kids would know to come to my house for Trick or Treat.

But, this being New York and the house being in a really nice neighborhood on the Upper West Side, the house is listed for over $10 million. And with the huge number of folks in this town with huge numbers of dollars to spend, it will move shortly into someone else's hands again.

If I win the Powerball, I will make them an offer. But if I don't, I hope the new owners treat it kindly. It's a hell of a nice house.

My Pre-War Bathrooms

When I bought my Pre-War, Art Deco, New York City apartment nearly five years ago, I toyed with the idea of updating my bathrooms. I have one full bath and one half bath. I consulted design magazines and home improvement TV shows about renovation, I went to Home Depot and Lowe's for inspiration, and I loved imagining new Art Deco fixtures and medicine cabinets to go with my classic Art Deco apartment. Then, I decided just to embrace 1941.

So, picture yourself in my apartment when it first went up. The Japanese had yet to bomb Pearl Harbor and our boys were still in school or at work and not yet on aircraft carriers in the South Pacific. FDR was president and the Bronx was home to large, New York families who loved the community and cheered for the Yankees. And somewhere in this idyllic landscape, somebody thought it would be a swell idea to install salmon pink and maroon bathrooms in every apartment in their new construction site.

Superficially, you could say, that's not such a big decision, after all, maroon is not a totally offensive color and a lot of neutral colors go with it. But in practice, what we have here is a symphony of maroon, a network of maroon, a veritable outrage of maroon. I have a maroon bathtub. I have maroon sinks. I have a full-sized, maroon shower stall. I probably had maroon toilets too, but they must have been replaced over the past 70-plus years by white ones.

Hear "maroon?" Think: dark blood red.

What goes with maroon? Well, if you are asking the guys who designed the fittings in this building, they must have all thought pink was the answer. And not the only answer, mind you. I have salmon tiles on the walls, framed with dark brown, not quite maroon tiles. I have pale pink and white tiles on the floor. When I had to paint the room, I was tempted to try another shade altogether, something in the blush range. But I caved and went with a pale gray. Nothing goes with maroon.

No Exit, or How It Took All Day to Fly for 38 Minutes

I hate flying with stopovers. I want to fly once in a day, not twice. I want to get from Point A to Point B, period. Don't try to amuse me with sprints through airport concourses and endless kiosks selling those dumb fuzzy neck pillows. I am not a cranky person, but making that second plane really brings out the worst. I am not a "stopping in the woods on a snowy evening" kind of a guy. I want to get right on through the woods and out to wherever I am going.

That's why I wait to fly to visit my family in the Midwest until April. I wait out the weather so I'm not stranded at tiny airports watching blizzards come and go, and I don't need my woolies in April. So I decided yesterday would be fine.

I got out of NYC on time, everything was good, and then I changed planes in Detroit. The incoming flight was delayed by about 15 minutes and I thought nothing about it until I saw the dead stares and sick faces of the passengers getting off our next plane. I heard the words "sick to my stomach," "Oh my God the turbulence," and "Thank God!" But I still thought nothing of it because I figured they were coming from Oklahoma or something, far, far away.

We get on the plane, I'm in Zone 1, I'm happy, it's 38 minutes in the air and we're done for the day. It was 79 degrees out. Then I knock my head into the overhead bin, sit down, curse a bit, and the man ahead of me accidentally grabs my foot as he lowers his arm rest.

We pull back about 10 feet from the gate and the pilot says, "There's a rain shower off to our left and we are going to just sit this out. We'll be going in about a half hour." I look at my phone, OK, don't rat me out, but I look at my phone and there's a tornado watch for the county until 6PM. And we are in a tiny, lightweight plane, sitting out, away from the gate, and the sky has gone black.

Great.

This is where it gets interesting. I had already given over my next half hour to the Fates when the woman sitting behind me starts panting, "I can't breathe, I can't breathe!" She was having a full-blown panic attack *and* she was holding an infant. The plucky newbie flight attendant with great Martha Graham-like body language rushes back (thunder, lightning, rain pelting the plane), and asks the mom if she wants to call the medics. We pull back to the gate, the medics come, they take the mom's pulse, they take the baby, and they exit, leaving us now back at the gate.

The storm passes. We don't get tossed into the air like toys, and we back away from the gate again to head out to join a now mile-long line to take off. There are 14 planes ahead of us, but that's all good, so I pull out my book.

We sit there for an hour, an hour 20 maybe. Then the pilot says, "We are having mechanical problems and will be going back to the gate. Either they will repair the issue or you will be put on another aircraft." Then, he floors it. I have flown lots of places, but he was just a few MPH from taking off. He careens around corners, he varooms us back to the gate, and he screeches to a halt while the ground crew scampers out to greet us. This takes another 20 minutes. It was a single, busted, windshield wiper that brought everything to a halt.

Now, we are back in the terminal trotting off to our next gate assignment where we board an identical plane and are seated in identical seats. This has the most amazing effect. It was like the Bill Murray movie, *Groundhog Day*. Once more, I knock my head into the overhead bin, sit down, curse a bit, and the man ahead of me accidentally grabs my foot as he lowers his arm rest. And I have just pulled up to the same Detroit Metro Airport terminal three times in one afternoon.

Visibility is now zero. It's pouring rain. So I put my next hour back in the hands of the Fates. Again the pilot floors it to get to the runway to take off. What was up with that?

A scant 38 minutes later we land in Indiana. We were supposed to have left Detroit at 1:55 p.m. We landed in Indiana at 8:00 p.m.

I would like to credit the plucky newbie flight attendant with the Martha Graham moves for making this trip less of an awful adventure and more like an interesting experience. She was our lone flight attendant through terrible weather, a sick passenger with a baby, twice returning to the gate, changing planes, and zero visibility – and she was great. She was so new she hadn't memorized the *spiel* yet and had to read the inflight safety instructions from a manual. But she bounced and she skipped down the aisle, and she was the consummate professional in the face of all that craziness. She was no-nonsense but with a wonderful sense of humor.

Hats off to you, Adriana on Flight 3663. You might have wanted to be a dancer, but yesterday, I was glad you were a flight attendant.

Oh yeah, it's 38 degrees out right now and there's snow in tonight's forecast.

In April.

Sausage Egg and Cheese

I walk down to the B train,
It's 8:22 crowded and
You are already there aloof,
Holding a free paper
And a sausage egg and cheese.

Dark clothes, comfortable shoes
Simply staring ahead,
Ignoring us all walking by you,
Nibbling on a fragrant, compelling
Sausage egg and cheese.

Tin foil cupped
Around the sliced white paper
As you take dainty bite after bite
Of that perfect
Sausage egg and cheese.

When the B train comes,
I leave you to find a seat near the door.
Leaving you standing there
Waiting for what?

Standing all alone on the platform now
With that sausage egg and cheese.

The mind is a fertile place at 8:22;
Open to suggestion,
Unable to resist.

I've been waylaid and Shanghaied
By a guy with a sandwich.
I've caught the baton,
And the relay continues.

And all I can think of
All I can do is count the stops
On this damn train til I can bag me
My own
Sausage -
Spicy hot tasty perfectly prepared,
Egg -
"Do you want salt and pepper?"
and,
"Is this to go?"
"Yes sir, it is, sir."
Cheese.

Age before Beauty?

I like to ride the subway at off hours, when it's not so crowded. This morning, I got on a fairly crowded train but saw some space next to a Lisbeth Salander type near the center of the train car. She was smallish, appropriately pierced and dark, and she was playing with her Blackberry so I took out my book and sat down.

On the other side of her, there was some space but not really enough for any average-sized grown-up, and a really huge man in a black coat – neither being unusual on the subway.

We pull into the next stop and little has changed. I am reading my book, Lisbeth is still playing with her Blackberry and I look up long enough to notice the huge man is now sound asleep. A woman gets on. She's carrying a fuchsia shoulder bag and she's fairly large, larger than me certainly, and she eyes the car, looking for a seat. Fuchsia Bag walks over to Lisbeth and motions to her that she would like to sit, but Lisbeth will not have it. She gives Fuchsia Bag a blank stare and says, "This isn't a seat, there's not enough space." Fuchsia Bag tries again: "I'd like to sit." But Lisbeth holds her own and goes back to playing.

I have just walked to the station from another borough, but I'd like to help out, so I ask the woman if she'd like my seat, would she like to sit down? She takes one step back, smiles at me, and delivers the death blow: "Oh my God, no. You're a lot older than I am!"

The train pulls out.

I don't remember seeing her leave.

When I get off the train, I buy myself a hot dog and try to recover a bit, but recovery is in short supply. Seven words from a stranger and I'm ready for a lap robe, a pot of tea, a handful of Snickerdoodles, and then, a nap.

The Communion of Saints

My three favorite holidays are Halloween, All Saints Day, and All Souls Day, which is also known as the Day of the Dead. I have come to appreciate these days more in recent years for a number of reasons, not the least of which is my new-found hobby: family history research. This hobby has brought me in and out of a dozen wonderful cemeteries, both here in the U.S. and in Ireland, and through these visits, I find myself now coming around to an understanding of a single line in a prayer I learned in the second grade.

"I believe in the communion of saints."

I have recited these lines, from memory, in complete oblivion all my life. They are nestled in and among some lovely words that I memorized in grade school, along with the Pledge of Allegiance and the Girl Scout Oath. The line never meant anything to me other than to suggest a certain reverence for the holy men and women who have been identified by the Catholic Church as saints. These are the people, all dead, who have made a spiritual impact on the living. They are remembered by their followers, their neighbors, their town.

But I have always thought of saints as separate from me, different from me, and better than me. Isn't that why we call them saints? They work miracles, they were strong, or devoted, or saintly in ways to which I can only aspire. In my dreams, I could be *like* a saint.

I visited the cemetery just a few weeks ago to see where my mother is buried. It's a small town cemetery for which I have always had a fondness because I recognize most of the names on the headstones. These are the graves of the mothers and fathers of the children from my school. It's not a particularly fancy place. There aren't any impressive monuments or large mausoleums, but my best friend from the eighth grade is there, so every time I would drive by, I'd think of her and smile, remembering how we spent time sledding in the winter or sharing bags of popcorn at the local movie house.

When I started collecting information about my father's family, I located a document that listed that very cemetery as the final resting place of his great aunt and her husband. I found their grave and added photos of the headstone to my family tree, all the while thinking how nice it would be if someone had photos of them, too, so I could get to know them a little better. My aunt died in 1938, so I considered the exercise a necessary yet lost cause.

Then, I thought, it was time I left some flowers as a tribute to my slim connection to this woman and her husband. I had given up the idea of ever knowing what she looked like and I knew very little about her, but I decided that pink carnations might be a fitting tribute. The color looked great against the gray stone, so I took another photo and left. The next day, I was looking around for old photos of the town and I stumbled upon a Facebook photo collection of the lake resort they had owned, where so many of my relatives had gone to dance. The photos were labeled "Grandmother." Her great-grandson – a cousin I had never met – had assembled and posted the collection.

It would be easy for me to say that her spirit led me to find this marvelous album of photos of her and her family. I could say there was some unseen force that motivated me to go to this particular site, looking for photos of the town and finding the very thing I had looked for, but that's not what this is about, I don't think.

Slowly, I am coming around to something my cousin said when I told her what had happened, how I had left the pink flowers and suddenly found the photos. I had given up ever finding images of this aunt and now, in a single flash, I had a dozen of them. She said simply, "I believe in the communion of saints."

And there we had it. Finally, and without realizing it, I had embraced the communion of saints. This communion is why I am drawn to cemeteries. This communion is why I find cathedrals and churchyards to be so peaceful and so calming.

It's much less about the Church and that prayer that I recited for so long and more about identifying the immutable connection between the living and dead. The departed souls we celebrate on the Day of the Dead are a real tangible part of this more abstract notion of a communion. We are all bound together by experience, by family, by loss, or by joy.

We are gathered together with similar threads and in that moment when I am standing in the midst of the dead, whether it is in that lovely small town graveyard, or an antique churchyard on a hill overlooking the Irish Sea, or the civic cemetery next to my bus stop in Manhattan, I can feel it.

The dead cannot judge you or hurt you. All that remains is the communion.

I believe in the communion of saints.

My Mother's Recipes

I think it's safe to say that the relationship you have with your mother is the single most complicated, complex, fascinating, and unique of all the interpersonal relationships in your life. I admit I have spent more time analyzing my relationship with my own mother since she died than I have since I was a teenager in the midst of the famous '60s "Generation Gap." It was never easy, it was rarely fulfilling, most of the conflict was my fault – but now that she is gone, may God have mercy on her soul, I've only got these small bits and pieces left. There are words, phrases, some sentences, few paragraphs. Relics.

And there are these recipes.

Much as I would like to be able now to distill my mother's cooking into a handful of adjectives, it's nearly impossible to do so. I have the sense that she really did not enjoy cooking and that if something weren't "quick and easy" as the old cookbook chapter headings said, it wasn't likely that particular dish would surface on a dinner table any time soon.

I remember she would call them hamburgers when we had the money for ground beef *and* bread, and meatballs, when we only had enough money for meat. I know she made spaghetti sauce from a box and that my dad wouldn't eat it the first day, only the second. I remember lots of Campbell's tomato soup, Velveeta or peach jam sandwiches on Fridays, and waffles on chilly mornings with Smoki-link sausages. She rarely ate what she served the rest of us, preparing her own large, fresh salad. It's funny that I never once ate a salad until I was out of college because, since she never served it to us, I figured it was something only grown-ups ate. She used to set our dinner on the table and place her salad bowl in front of her. She always had iceberg lettuce, fresh tomato, cucumber, onion, and green pepper kept in the bottom drawer of the refrigerator. She called it the "crisper."

When I went away to school, she took the time to

type up a handful of recipes to give me so I would have something to cook out on my own. I always thought these recipes, which I had not looked at for years until just a few days ago, were something she cooked for us when I was a kid. But it turns out, now that I read them, she hadn't made most of them. They are prefaced with "I haven't tried this one" or "I know someone who tried this and liked it."

There is only one of them, the family recipe for Beef Stew, that I remember eating as a child and that I have started making again as an adult. It tastes exactly the way I remember it and it is very reminiscent of the Irish stews I tried in Ireland when I was there a couple of years ago. It is simple, quick, nearly foolproof, and delicious. But at the end of the typing, she wrote "This is not so quick and easy."

So, here I am now, just a few years after her death, trying to piece together something that I can hang onto that spoke of my mother. She didn't leave me any objects, like jewelry or a lamp. She didn't leave me money or property. I've got a mirror that is in one of her wedding day pictures, a dress, and a random assortment of photographs. But these recipes can live off the page once they are cooked and it's something real. There's magic in cooking that I usually take for granted. In this case though, I really sense the magic and the few memories I have of my mother in the kitchen at home come back to me when I make this stew.

I am not prompted to make all of these recipes because frankly, neither was she. But I want my children to think of this elusive woman when I make her Beef Stew.

And maybe someday, with their own children, they'll also think of me.

Looking for Crocus

It is difficult to say now, but my mother and I were never really close after I left the Midwest to live in New York. I wanted her to call me more often but was never sure what I wanted her to say, and I'm sure she wanted to call me but couldn't find a way through to do it. I have some of her recipes and a handful of notes she wrote to my children years ago, but there's not much more now that she's gone.

And yet, I will always remember my mother in the spring. She had a particular fondness for spring that I think said a lot about her eagerness to throw off winter sooner than everyone else.

My mother loved crocus shoots. No matter where we were, she would always point out the "green, growing things," as she called them. It got to the point where I would look for patches of green through all the snow that piled up near our house in Michigan in late winter, hoping to catch a groundhog-like glimpse of something that promised us a proximity to spring.

My mother grew the daintiest white Lilies of the Valley in the back yard, next to my father's spiky chives. The plants, much like my parents, were the perfect pair. Flowers meant something to my mother. She had dozens of "Four O'Clocks," twin rose bushes – one white and one red – and she loved flowering shrubs: Rose of Sharon, Forsythia, Lilacs. She bought dozens of tulips in Holland, Michigan and planted them in the front yard.

For my parents' 50th wedding anniversary, I bought them a red bud tree, one of the most beautiful of the flowering trees that will survive Michigan winters. In the spring, that tree blooms with flowers that are caught somewhere between lavender and fuchsia. The small clutches of flowers are set off against the nearly black bark of the slender trees and they will always catch your attention when you drive by houses with red buds planted in the yard.

There is a wonderful drive which we took on Sundays

when I was little along the Red Bud Trail where you can watch these beautiful trees in bloom in groves along the river not too far from our house.

It's funny now when I think about her, as I look for crocus and green, growing things. I never thought of my mother as an outdoors type. She grew up in a big city and even though she spent much more time in our small town than she lived in the city as a girl, I never associated her with gardens, yet now, as I think about her, I don't think of alleys and concrete, I think of shrubs and flowers. There was something about the change of winter into spring that captivated her. She didn't drive when I was really small, so maybe she looked forward to walking on clean sidewalks that weren't icy-challenging or maybe she tired of the extra blankets and sweaters that we needed to stay warm. In my thoughts, I see her face now looking into the sunlight, waiting, watching for some sign that winter is finished and the gray skies are behind her.

My mother was 92 years old when she died. Our relationship was cluttered with sarcasm and disappointment scattered over the years much the same way closets get when you don't take the time to sort things out. But I will look for the crocus every spring and think of her. I can still smell her Lilies of the Valley and I will always look for green, growing things through the piles of snow.

If she taught me anything, it was to embrace hope.

The Black Sheep

My mother thrived in captivity.
Surrounded by her books and shawls,
Her tea steaming alongside her on the lamp table,
Fresh white flowers in a cut glass vase.

Safe,
Sometimes dozing, sometimes sharing what she read,
Wrapped in words,
Her stories taking her through history and places far away.
Thoughts collected on her journeys,
A sentence here or there,
Like souvenirs packed in a well-worn trunk,
Or displayed in a vitrine in the hall.
Never leaving, always traveling.
Safe.

I chose the west wind to comb my hair.
The antique ferns standing at attention
Along the way, as I pass.
Dust and gravel, small stones beneath my feet,
And the sound of tall trees whispering beside me
Or of thick rain dropping on red flowers
Just-blooming at the edge of a farmer's field.
Cloud canopy and a cold stone bench,
Solitary.

I am my father's daughter.

Memento

Sur la place chacun passe, chacun vient, chacun va;
*Drôles de gens que ces gens-là!**

My mother was a singer. She never sang for money and for the life of me, I don't remember her ever singing alone in front of people, not even at Christmas when everyone sang carols in both English and Latin. My great aunt would get tipsy and sing everyone else under the table, but not my mother. She only sang to us.

When I was little, we had a bed time that was fixed in stone. There was a routine of picking up our things, saying prayers, getting under the covers, and listening to my mother's stories and her nightly song list. It was part 1940s hit parade, part Irish folk songs and to this day, I can still hear her singing "Galway Bay." I was spoiled beyond description.

My mother's musical taste was incredibly vast and completely indiscriminate. She and I would take records out of the local public library and play them over and over, then return them, only to check them out again. This is how I was able to memorize the original cast recordings of every major Broadway musical of the 1960s, including *The Sound of Music*, *The Music Man*, *Brigadoon*, *Camelot*, and *My Fair Lady* and I sang them until I had every breath, every nuance down cold. If there ever was a Broadway baby, it was me, even though, at the time, I was living in southwestern Michigan and wouldn't find my way to New York until I was in graduate school.

My mother could quote Gilbert and Sullivan operettas, she knew the names of every John Philip Sousa march and Strauss waltz, she adored Mariachis, and she loved opera, even though at that time, it was a serious logistical challenge to attend live performances. For me, growing up, opera was just another colorful patch in her musical quilt. The music my mother loved embraced me. It shored me up at times and insulated and protected me at others. It was my soft comfort on a difficult day, a friend who never judged me unless I gave in to a distraction and forgot the words to the song.

When I was ten, the New York City Opera touring company came to a local auditorium with a performance of Bizet's opera, *Carmen*. My mother bought tickets and I remember sitting close to the stage, ecstatic to be able to hear live playing and singing. I sat transfixed and burst into tears when Carmen was stabbed to death by Don Jose. I went to school the next day and told everyone I wanted to take the name of Carmen for my upcoming Confirmation. My mother was horrified, so we struck a bargain and I agreed to downsize to Carmel, after the Irish singer, Carmel Quinn.

But the die was cast. By the time I graduated from college, I had sung in the church choir, in summer stock, in glee club in high school, in a local coffee house, and in three different university chorus organizations. I sang with guitar, with piano, by myself, with my friends. To me, singing was like a rare, really expensive designer high. The more I performed, the more I needed to do it. If I wasn't cast in something, I would volunteer to usher. I'd sew costumes, hang gels in the light fixtures, or design makeup just to stay in the theater. I auditioned for the college opera company where I sang in four operas in three semesters, netting me three credits in music that I applied to my undergraduate degree. Other people were writing papers for their three credits – I was singing.

Amateur singing was my gateway drug. Now, I just wasn't satisfied: I needed more. A friend of mine told me about a church choir in Chicago that paid its singers and a few days later, I was in. It was my first professional choir, made up of 15 other singers and accompanied in concerts by a sweet little pick-up band called the Hyde Park Chamber Orchestra.

That little band was made up of many of the first chairs of the Chicago Symphony and when they played *Messiah*, we singers were transported and none of us could talk about it much for hours afterwards. I have no recordings from any of those concerts, but even a professional recording would not do justice to the chills we all got from that five note trumpet solo three quarters of the way through the *Hallelujah* chorus.

Still not enough. I understudied the role of Carmen at a local opera company, bought my own recordings, started to study more seriously, audition more frequently, sing more often. I was fearless. I don't think I have ever sung the National Anthem as a soloist, but I have sung weddings, funerals, oratorios, recitals, symphony choruses, and dozens of solos. I have sung in English certainly, but also French, German, Italian, Spanish, Czech, Russian, Venetian dialect, and old English.

I spent a summer working as an apprentice in an American opera company and another summer, I lived in a Belgian castle in a suite I decorated with fresh-picked poppies. We sang opera excerpts on the radio broadcast of the opening of the Festival of Flanders. I toured Italy with an American chorus in an Italian opera company and sang with a string quartet at a Sunday afternoon concert in Spoleto. My name was in the headline of the newspaper review.

But in all this, I can safely say the highlight, the pinnacle, the very highest high was in Siena, Italy nearly 30 years ago. I'm tempted to qualify this moment by downgrading the impact of the actual event, but I wouldn't be doing it justice. Simply put, I was just working with a classical guitar player. We'd been rehearsing some old English songs and a handful of great Scarlatti arias with a wonderful flute player and we had the pieces of a very compelling recital coming together slowly. The director of the company interrupted our plan by offering me the chance to tour Tuscany with a full set of Federico Garcia Lorca songs. It would be singing in Spanish – just the guitar player and me.

It was late in July. Siena was preparing for the second Palio and that summer had record-breaking heat. We rehearsed in the late afternoon in hot rehearsal rooms until I knew we could do those songs anywhere. I performed them many times in piazzas and in churches, each performance more assured and confident than the last. In that moment, I knew of no singer who could touch me in this repertoire.

I had a good friend with me that summer who knew a local bistro owner. He convinced him to let me sing the songs at the restaurant, after it had closed for the night, roughly 2:00 a.m. For some reason, none of the formal performances we had turned out appealed to me as much as this chance to sing in a local place. I would be surrounded by his neighbors, his friends, his family and I wanted to be wonderful.

My guitarist wanted to rehearse at the same time of day, 2:00 a.m., so we could anticipate the actual performance. The rehearsal rooms were all closed for the night, so he decided we'd sit out on his balcony, in the moonlight, in the dying heat of that day in July. He started to play so softly I could barely hear him and in that moment, it was as if we were sitting together outside Granada in Spain with Lorca himself.

I started to sing, cautiously at first, from verse to chorus to verse again. I knew we needed to work, but it was late and I didn't want his neighbors to complain. I sang to him as my mother used to sing to me, softly, with tremendous caring. And when I finished the song, we heard applause. His neighbors were listening to us. By the time we had finished the set, the applause came from balconies and windows all around us and the moon was full overhead.

The next night we performed at the bistro. I sat in the open window of the restaurant and my guitarist sat at one of the tables. The restaurant was filled with the owner's friends. The street was filled with his neighbors. I remember it so clearly. It was extraordinary.

*Libretto, Henri Meilhac and Ludovic Halévy, *Carmen,* Act I

To Laugh

I started to write about two young women
in a black and white photograph;
they are sitting together on a porch.

It is Easter and a baby sits between them,
a full woven basket on his lap,
long sleeves, long skirts, button shoes.

They are carefree and breezy, and hopelessly demure.
And I think of my Easters, too.

Dressing up for spring, taking photos of everyone
Smiling, standing in front of new flowers.

But I am distracted and the photo fades
and I can only think of you now:
and the way you made me feel safe enough
to laugh.

Misty for Me

It just wasn't what Mark wanted.

Mark had been an orchestra conductor all his life, leading his friends in small afternoon get-togethers at his mother's house, putting together string ensembles in high school, anything for the sound of applause and a chance to step away from the podium and take a bow. There was something so thrilling to him when he could turn to the concertmaster and offer him his hand. He could play every instrument in the orchestra and had soloed in viola competitions since music camp.

So how was it, he wondered to himself as he left the school auditorium, that he was still playing these tired gigs with community pick-up orchestras in Vermont every year?

Mark thanked the stage hands as he left the stage. They were taking down the music stands, folding up the chairs, collecting the sheet music. Mark tucked his score into his briefcase and waved a silent *Ciao-ciao* goodnight to the theater doorman, walking through the alley behind the theater and into the now empty street.

There was only one bar still open at this hour and he just wanted to stop in for a drink and to have a moment to feel sorry for himself. It was a regular kind of a place where everyone really did know your name, with a roughed up spinet piano in the back next to the pool table and a couple of small, two-chair tables along the exposed brick wall opposite the bar. Mike was long gone, retired, but his son, Charlie, ran the place.

Charlie watched Mark come in. Mark smiled and walked toward the back and sat down next to an old red and silver juke box.

"Whaddya have, Maestro?" Mark squirmed at that name.

How terribly inappropriate, he thought to himself, given tonight's lackluster performance and the grim thought of having to repeat it for the next two nights' running.

"Well, sir, normally I would have my regular '78 Dom Perignon, but tonight is special, I think. Give me your best draught and we'll call it a day, my friend."

The bartender squirmed at *that*. He pulled a clean glass out of the tray, fresh from the dishwasher. Cold beer filled the glass. He picked up a couple of cocktail napkins and walked the beer back to Mark's table.

It was late. The last two guys at the bar were settling up their tab and packing it in for the night. Charlie placed the tall glass on the small table.

"So where's that good looking girl singer I saw you with? She meeting you here?"

Bartenders don't always like to pry, but for some reason, since the place was quiet, Charlie thought he'd make the effort at conversation. Not friends, of course, just making the effort.

"Oh, you mean, Mary? The soprano from Wing Lake? She left the theater just before I did. To be honest, I thought she might be here."

Just then, a slim brunette opened the door and was swept into the bar by the breeze from the street. It was starting to get colder, cold for August at least, and she was wrapped in a silvery gray Pashmina. The light from the ceiling fan caught the red glints in her hair. She was still wearing concert dress and her stilettos clacked on the wood floor of the bar as she made her way to the back. It was as if she knew Mark was there before she entered the room.

"Hello," she said slowly. "I thought I'd find you here. Drowning sorrows, are we? Something about the band, I would presume, and not my performance, I hope?"

Mary slid the Pashmina off her shoulders and onto the back of the chair, revealing the whitest skin Mark had ever seen. He had known Mary since they were students together at the Manhattan School of Music. To make money to pay for his studio rentals, Mark would play piano for the voice teachers' singing lessons and he loved playing for Mary's. He always envisioned her singing him to sleep.

Mary sat in the chair and their game of Cat and Mouse continued.

"Can an old friend buy an old friend a drink? I'll pick up the tab on your beer there, or we can get you something more interesting. Absinthe, perhaps? Or maybe arsenic? Something more fitting?"

"I'm fine with the beer. And I'll let you pick up the tab on one condition. Stay and have a drink with me, right here, right now, and agree to the condition without knowing what it is. Otherwise I'm buying my own beer. Game, *mia bella*, Maribella?"

The sound of that name shot right through her. He hadn't called her that since that night in Rome so many years ago. They had toured with an ensemble, he conducting, she singing, and he started calling her *mia bella* Maribella. She could almost hear the sound of the birds in the trees outside their Italian apartment, the one in the palazzo with the swirling stone staircase and the icy marble floors.

"Deal," she replied.

She turned to Charlie and said, "Give me a Scotch neat, *per favore*, and I guess we'll see what kind of condition we are in for afterwards."

Charlie walked back to the bar.

"Am I allowed to ask questions, or will the condition be revealed like the end of some mystery game?"

Mary set her purse on the table. Mark started inching his index finger around the rim of the Pilsner glass in front of him. He was thinking.

Mark stood up and walked to the juke box and scanned the tunes through the glass front. He looked back at her and smiled, then turned back to the juke box. Charlie brought her the Scotch.

"How about some music, Maribella?"

Mark fished some coins out of his pants pocket and punched in the tune. He turned and held out his hand. Mary shook her head at Mark.

"You cannot be serious! You really want to dance

with me, here, now, and me in these heels?"

He walked back to the table, never dropping his hand to her, as the music started to play and he took a quick drink of his beer. She finished the Scotch and stood up, taking his hand, pausing for a moment to slip her feet out of her satin shoes. He pulled her away from the table and into his arms. The song was "Misty."

Mark said nothing to her. He pulled her close and pressed his hand against the small of her back, drinking in her perfume, burying his face in her hair. She pulled back.

"Look, Mark, I want to say something, something about Rome," Mary started.

He put two fingers across her lips and started singing to her. His eyes never left hers.

"Look at me," he started to sing softly, all the while moving her around the floor, "I get misty just holding your hand."

When the music ended, there was a complete, filled silence surrounding the two dancers. Charlie had stopped washing up to watch them, and it seemed like the conductor and his muse were alone in the world they had created.

Without a word, Mark and Mary walked slowly back to the table. He leaned over to pick up his briefcase and offered Mary her Pashmina.

"Better pay the man, Maribella. I'm taking you home."

Mary pulled two fives out of her purse and left them on the table.

"So, are you going to tell me the condition now, Mark, *before* you have your way with me?"

She had that sly smile on her face that he remembered so well. She stepped back into her shoes.

"One dance," he said to her. "That's all I wanted. I never asked to have my way with you, now did I?"

Charlie was done mopping up the bar. He switched off the ceiling fan, and picked up his keys to close up. Mark and his beautiful Maribella walked out together into the chill of the night. She leaned against his arm and began humming softly. They sang the chorus together, just walking up the street.

To Dance

What if you asked me to dance?
Would you see that I don't know how?
Would you feel me resist when you offer your hand?
Would you sense my fear
as you placed your arm around my back?

We're talking
saying nothings
not listening to each other
but the music.

Please let me sit down.
I'm embarrassed, exposed,
I'm afraid.
All bravado with no substance as we move together,
All silk and feathers' essence as the music plays
and the players ignore us.

I want to beg you to let me stop
but I can't say anything now
because the dance
the dancing
the dancing with you
takes hold
and I understand that I knew how to dance all along.

It's just today
I am learning
how to dance
with
you.

Bright Angel Feet

"Shall we gather at the river, the beautiful, the beautiful river? Gather with the saints, hmm, hmm, that flows, hmm, hmm, God."

Molly was singing to herself, toweling off after her shower. An early morning run had her thinking of her day, wondering if that 25% chance of rain meant it really would rain. Umbrella, no umbrella?

"I think I need to be prepared," she said to herself in the mirror. "I am taking my new smiley face umbrella to go with my kicky yellow rain boots and my brand new slicker hat."

Walking out of the apartment building, she nodded and smiled to the porter who was taking out the recyclables, reminding him to "Have a blessed day."

He grimaced at the weight of the clear plastic bag and nodded back. His not speaking a word of English was not going to get her down today. She just skipped up the steps and walked out into the morning light, not a cloud in the sky.

Molly walked down the block to the bus station, greeting and smiling all the way.

"Have a blessed day, everyone," she waved into the open door of the Twin Donut Shop on the corner, and even though nobody there spoke English either, they understood her wave and her cheery smile. They all waved back, smiling, muttering something about *gringa* under their breath.

Molly headed across the street to the stop and she watched as a bus pulled up. Molly just smiled as she slipped into a seat near the window. She pulled a dog-eared copy of the New Testament out of her bag and started mouthing the words to John Chapter 14:6. And she started humming again, the smile never leaving her face as the nearly empty bus started across the avenue and onto the bridge.

At the first stop, Molly noticed two young men walking together on their way to school, looking like Frank Sinatra without the fedora, their school uniform blazers slung over their shoulders. Instead of thinking of the day they would have, learning new things, meeting new people, trying new ideas out on their friends, Molly reflected on how lost young people are nowadays; how deluded, misguided, and confused.

She went back to her John 14:6, vowing to pray for them all just as soon as she could.

At the next stop, she collected her things and gave her little New Testament a kiss as she put it into her bag and prepared to get off the bus. The driver turned off the highway and onto a side street, but since Molly had been so distracted watching the boys this morning, she had forgotten to signal her stop and missed it altogether, the bus moving quickly down the block and away from her office. *No bother*, she thought.

They tell you to get out and get more exercise and today, the Good Lord gave me that opportunity, she thought to herself. She thanked the driver and started walking back up the block to her office.

"The beautiful, the beautiful river, shall we gather, hmm, hmm."

Molly opened the door, walked across the lobby and took the elevator up to the agency. Molly walked out of the elevator, her jingling, smiley-face key ring in her hand.

At the front desk, a busy-looking woman saluted her with her coffee cup, the one with the yellow flowers on it.

"Hey, Stacey," Molly approached her. "How was your weekend? Did you get to the movies?"

Molly and Stacey met in middle school. They sat next to each other in Advanced Math 2. They had worked together at the agency since high school, Molly now sitting in the corner office, Stacey still working reception at the front desk.

Stacey took a sip of her coffee.

"I went with the kids to see that new Pixar movie, the one with the girl who does archery? They loved it. We went in the morning. Did you know you can get in for half price in the morning? We love to get in for half price. But the popcorn's still so expensive."

Stacey went on, "Especially when I take the girls. Neal stayed home with the twins. Neal Junior had a low fever and I didn't want to risk it."

"I always bring my own popcorn to the movies," Molly told her. "I'm on a tight budget, you know. I'm sorry – I forgot to give you the free passes I get every time from the theater company."

Stacey winced.

"Right," Stacey answered her, setting her coffee down to give Molly her mail. "You did have a couple of calls this morning. One from Prewitt, looking for a new face, and one from that guy who shot the promo. He didn't remember if it was you or Sam he worked with last week. Here are the numbers."

"Thanks, Stace. I'll be in my office. Actually, I'm expecting Mr. Prewitt."

Stacey waited until Molly had left and then she rolled her eyes and sat down to finish her now lukewarm coffee. She pulled one of her daughter's stuffed Happy Meal toys out of her desk drawer and promptly stapled its stomach to its back and dropped it back into her drawer. She'd done it before when Molly's cheery attitude was more than she could stand and she knew that it was better to deploy a stapler than a sharp retort or a hand gun.

Just then the elevator doors opened and Robbie Prewitt stepped out, looking stunning. Everything matched: his makeup was perfect, new shoes were clean, and a cape dragged across his shoulders draped and fell with architectural precision. He wore fuchsia socks and his black shoes were as shiny as a Marine's dress uniform.

Mr. Prewitt swept across the lobby and stood tall in front of her desk, giving Stacey a look that said, "I know I know you from somewhere, wait, don't remind me." She recognized that look and didn't remind him she'd worked the front desk at his agency for the past nine years.

Molly came out to usher Mr. Prewitt into her office,

greeting him with a big smile and a small, ineffective handshake, as she offered to take his cape. Mr. Prewitt declined, his heels clicking on the polished floor. He took a chair at the head of the conference table where tall glasses and a pitcher of ice water were waiting for them.

"We are looking for a face and an idea, Molly, and I expect you to deliver." Mr. Prewitt started right in. Molly sat down next to him, offering the pitcher, but again Mr. Prewitt declined her offer. "You remember the last one? Now that was something!"

Molly looked out the window. She was waiting for a miracle. She was waiting for inspiration. And she was waiting for Stacey's routine "in five minutes, just save me" phone call.

Ring, ring.

"Please excuse me, Mr. Prewitt, I need to take this call. Hello? Yes, yes? No! OK. I'll be right out. Thanks." Turning to Mr. Prewitt, Molly said, "I'm sorry, sir. I just need to step out for a second, may I?"

Mr. Prewitt nodded and Molly stepped out, closing the door behind her. She leaned on the door and ran through all the faces she could call up without her book in front of her. Sydney was getting old, Madison was out of town, Dylan was already working in Florida, and Heather, who knew what was going on with Heather? Where was she going to find the new face, the one that would fill the bill and then some?

Molly opened the door again and took her seat at the conference table, smiling, apologizing. Mr. Prewitt breathed in noisily to cut her off and asked, "Well?"

"I do have an idea," Molly said. "I would like to try something new, something fresh. Would you be willing to take a chance, maybe gamble on a sure thing? I think this could be big."

Mr. Prewitt picked up his bag. "Molly, you have never let us down before. Have your idea on my desk by the end of next week. And if you need to take a couple of days off between now and then, well, you go right ahead."

He gathered up his cape and reached for Molly's hand

on her way out, shaking it firmly before walking out the door into the corridor toward the elevators. The two of them were standing next to Stacey's desk at reception in the lobby now.

"I'll drop the keys to my Hamptons house into the mailbox by the gate. You can just let yourself in and I'll let my cook and my driver know to expect you. Oh hell, why don't I just tell him to swing by your place and pick you up, save you that endless wait for the jitney?"

"Why thank you, Mr. Prewitt. You have a blessed day, sir!" Molly went back into her office to get her umbrella and her kicky boots. She was going to take the rest of the day off to work on her idea and rest up for the long drive to the Hamptons.

On her way out, Molly beamed at Stacey, who was about to start her day of filing, data entry, phone calls, supplies ordering, and mail sorting. Stacey picked up the phone to avoid talking to Molly and she reached back into her drawer for that toy she had stapled. Molly was about to wish her another blessed day, but Stacey missed it. She had her back to the lobby and she was concentrating on her stapling.

Just as she reached the lobby, Molly felt a queer, sharp-stabbing twinge in her stomach, something she'd felt before, but, thinking it was probably nothing, she continued out of the building, walking briskly and with purpose. She didn't need that umbrella after all.

Molly sang, "Where bright angel feet have trod, hmm, hmm by the river that flows hmm, hmm crystal tide forever, flowing by the throne of God."

Then she disappeared into the crowd on the street.

Back upstairs, Stacey was just finishing up an urgent phone call from Neal. She was alone in the reception area, staring ahead of her, across the partition that ran along the front of her desk, separating the greeter from the greeted.

She gathered up the photographs of the kids and her hand lotion and dropped them into her bag. She had a curious smile on her face as she walked down to the conference room and looked in for just a second before shutting out the lights and calling the elevator to go down to the street. The security guard looked up.

"Hey, Stacey, anything wrong?" He stepped in front of her to open the door.

Stacey leaned over on tiptoes to give him a little smooch on the cheek.

"Nothing wrong, Richie, nothing at all. Remember me telling you Neal's great uncle died? Well, they read the will today and oh my God, we own the agency now! The whole damn thing. Prewitt's going to be working for me!"

Richie shouted "Congratulations! But hey, what about Molly?"

He called after her, but Stacey? Stacey had left the building.

The Staten Island Ferry

"Honey, grab the map, OK? This is going to be fun!"

Sandy put her sweater in her shoulder bag, picked up the room key card, and leaned over to give her new hubby a peck on the cheek.

"Shouldn't we just stick to midtown, you know, maybe get something to eat at Red Lobster before the show tonight?" Richard turned off the TV.

"What does the guidebook say again?" Sandy tossed the book on the bed.

"My grandfather says Staten Island is the best thing. It's supposed to be a place where the tourists don't go and you can get real good Italian food like in the movie, you remember, that one with, what was her name again? It had Alec Baldwin when he was a lot younger and," she made a face, "a lot thinner."

Richard shrugged. "You *know* I never remember that kind of thing! That's why I married you, Sandy Cakes." He picked up the guidebook and shut out the lights.

Richard and Sandy asked the hotel doorman to hail them a cab to the ferry landing. They slipped him a fresh dollar bill and settled in the back seat for the ride downtown. Sandy opened the guidebook.

"It says here that the Staten Island Zoo has a new snake exhibit. I like snakes, you like snakes. This is cool and everybody will love our pictures of snakes and it'll be great!"

Richard smiled and went back to looking out the window of the cab. As they arrived at the ferry terminal, he paid the driver, thanked him, and held the car door open for Sandy. They walked toward the ferry terminal and looked at the schedule. A ferry had just arrived, so they walked over to it and waited in the line.

"Oh, Richard, that's the Statue of Liberty! My grandfather used to tell us about coming to America and seeing it for the first time when he arrived from Italy. He lived on Staten Island for a while before moving to Indiana with my grandmother. I feel like I could be standing right next to him. Take my picture, OK? With the Statue in the background. He'll love it!"

Richard aimed his camera and Sandy smiled. He tucked the camera back in his jacket pocket just as the line started to board. They stepped onto the ferry, taking two seats near the window.

Sandy leaned over to the woman sitting across from her. Richard started to motion to her not to engage the woman in conversation, but Sandy wasn't paying attention.

"We're from Indiana. Have you been to Staten Island before?"

Sandy nodded with encouragement, expecting a response from the woman. The woman was wearing a long black dress with a soft black shawl that was more for decoration than use. She was carrying a small leather satchel with brass fittings and she sat leaning over her bag, slowly fingering a linen handkerchief. She barely looked up when Sandy started talking to her.

"No English," the woman whispered to Sandy. "I, no English."

Sandy looked at Richard. Undeterred, Sandy tried again, only much louder this time.

She shouted, "We're newlyweds! Have you been to Staten Island before?"

The woman also tried again.

"I, no English," she said. "*Italiano*."

Sandy lit up. Lowering her voice to a normal volume, she said to the woman, "Oh, my God, I speak Italian! My grandfather taught me."

"*Io parlo italiano, signora*."

The woman stopped playing with the handkerchief and looked up at Sandy with a quizzical smile. She held out her hand and said simply, "*Piacere*. Pleased to meet you."

"Oh, Richard, this is great. I'm making a friend, a friend from the Staten Island ferry." Richard just rolled his eyes and smiled at her.

Sandy spoke to the woman again. "*Signora*, my grandfather came to America from Siena and he came to Staten Island. We're just here to see the snakes though. At the zoo. My name is Sandy, *Alessandra*. Alessandra Donofrio. Well, now it's Alessandra Peters. We live in Indiana. *Piacere, signora, molto piacere*."

The woman picked up her bag and sat down between Richard and Sandy. She patted Sandy's hand.

"You remind me of someone, *ragazza*. Your grandfather, he was from Italy, *sì*?"

Sandy gasped. "Yes, *sì*! Do you know him?"

"My family lived next door to the Donofrios. We lived near the Cathedral. We went to Mass together every Sunday. Have you been there? To Siena?"

The woman was speaking slowly enough for Sandy to translate. "It is very beautiful there, very beautiful."

Sandy grabbed Richard's arm. "We were there on our honeymoon just last week, *signora*. It is very beautiful. Oh, Richard, take our picture together, please?"

The woman watched intently as Richard took his brand new Nikon out of his jacket. It was a wedding present from his uncle. He snapped a couple of shots as they made their way to the exit.

"May we take you somewhere please, *signora*?" Sandy wanted to help.

"I invite you to my home. After your snakes, of course."

"I would like that," Sandy answered her. "*Mille grazie, signora, mille grazie*. Where should we meet you?"

The ferry touched the pier and the woman appeared to lose her balance for an instant, pressing into Richard to steady herself, apologizing in Italian. She quickly tucked something into her bag and withdrew the linen hankie.

"It's not far, but you will have to take the bus to Old Ocean Drive. I will have a nice wine for you to try."

Richard helped her into a cab and was about to pay the driver a twenty. The woman waved goodbye and the cab took off. Sandy was ecstatic. Richard reached for his wallet.

"See, Richard? We've already made a friend in Staten Island. On Ocean Drive. Wait, what was her name?"

Richard patted his jacket pocket and then looked at Sandy.

"Honey? Have you seen my wallet?"

Lucy's Coffee Pot Retires

"Oh, Chock Full O' Nuts is the heavenly coffee," he sang softly to himself. "Better coffee a millionaire's money, oh yeah, his money, his money can't buy-ee!"

It was a morning like any morning. The sun coming up, just heard the alarm go off, and Coffee Pot smiled because breakfast with Lucy is most definitely the best part of waking up.

"I'm ready for anything," he whispered to himself. "Hazelnut, French Vanilla, Trader Joe's Colombian, oh, it's gonna be a great day!"

Waiting for his filter, his morning paper as he liked to call it, was always the hardest part. The sights, the sounds were all so familiar. The sound of the door closing to the bathroom was first. Well, it came first after that irritating alarm and that idiot radio that goes on and on with the stupid Light FM nonsense Lucy loves. But it's familiar and at this hour, that's not a bad thing, all in all, not a bad thing at all.

"Singing in the bathtub, la-de-da-de-da."

He heard the splish-splash of the water in her shower. It would be just a few more minutes until show time!

"Oh, la-de-da-de-da."

There's the bathroom door again and the swishing of the towels. Any minute now, any minute now, and we'll be ready to go. There's her shoes. He loves the sound of her shoes. There's something about that first thud, thud, and then the ticking of her heels across the floor. She'll be out in the kitchen soon, any minute now, and he was happily waiting for her.

"You light up my life, you give me hope to carry on," Lucy sang as she was gearing up for breakfast, singing along with her nonsense radio. He sat patiently, waiting for her to come into the kitchen and start her breakfast routine.

"Hey there, Coffee Pot!"

She ticked into the kitchen, blew two kisses at him, and opened the cupboard.

He knew her routine by heart. She was going to bring him the paper next, so he smiled to himself, waiting.

"Oh, no morning paper for you today, old friend," she said to him as she reached into the dishwasher for her favorite travel mug.

He thought to himself. "Wait, what the hell does that mean, no paper? That's not funny. We've had breakfast together for years and it's always started with my paper. She can't be serious. It's the way we've always done it. I wait. I listen, she does the shower, the shoes, and the songs on the radio. I get the paper and we have our moment. It doesn't last, but it's our moment."

"So, Coffee Pot, I want you to meet my new breakfast buddy, Mr. Keurig. I'm going to send you to my brother's house tonight when I get home from work. I know this is abrupt, but he'll just love you and it's time for you to retire. His old coffee pot broke yesterday and since I have my new Keurig machine, I just don't need to keep you here."

Now he was shouting to himself! "No! She's just going to give me away like last year's Coach bag? Oh hell, no!"

"Look, little buddy," she said as she unplugged the coffee pot cord and wound it around her hand. "Frank will just love you. And I will pack up all your stuff, the Chock Full O' Nuts coffee, the little dipper, and those nice, brown, recycled paper filters you love. You know, your 'morning paper'?"

He was crushed.

Lucy picked up the coffee pot and placed it gently into the bottom of a Whole Foods shopping bag. She dropped the paper filters and the rest of the stuff in beside it and set the bag on the floor by the front door.

"Oh, don't look so glum, old chum. I'll come visit." Lucy looked into the bag, arranging the bits and pieces of coffee paraphernalia.

She ticked back to the kitchen and selected a dark roast coffee K-Cup and set it on the counter next to the new coffee machine. She turned on the water in the sink and let it run until it was icy cold.

"You light up my life!"

She started singing again to herself as she pulled the toaster off the shelf over the counter and popped in two slices of whole wheat bread. She pulled a short strip of some Reynolds Wrap out of the drawer and set it next to the toaster.

Coffee Pot sat at the bottom of the Whole Foods bag.

"What is she thinking?"

"She'll come around."

"It's just a fad."

"The thing's got no staying power."

"She'll come back to me."

"Come back to me!"

She filled the reservoir and brewed her coffee, using her travel mug. The toast popped up and she wrapped the two pieces and dropped them into her purse.

He waited, sitting quietly in the bottom of the Whole Foods bag. This is not how his morning was supposed to go.

"Ciao, Coffee Pot. I'll be back later to take you to Frank's. You'll love it there. He's got lots of cats and he only makes coffee on the weekends!"

And then she was gone.

Coffee Pot heard Lucy tick down the hall.

"You light up my days, and fill my nights with song!"

"This is what they mean when they say to wake up and smell the coffee, I guess," he thought to himself.

"Wait! Are you kidding me? He's got cats?!"

Midnight Blue

It was just a day.

Some random Thursday in August, when I was on my way to work and waiting on the train platform at Rockefeller Center in Manhattan. Four trains stop on this platform and mine typically comes right in once I get there. But that morning, I found myself standing a while, then taking a seat on one of the long, divided wooden benches, then standing again, distracted. I was looking for inspiration, something to write about, something to say. I'd been working on some new poetry but it wasn't going well.

My train pulled in and emptied most of the passengers out into the station. I got on one of the middle cars and sat next to the door. Just across from me a man wearing a tan jacket was playing a game on his phone, a dozing student was holding a red canvas Verizon shopping bag, a woman across the way was feverishly highlighting passages in her book, and a mom sat next to her daughter. They were probably on their way to school.

As I sat there, I wondered what it would be like if some fanciful creature were suddenly to step onto the train. I've been focusing my writing on sensory things lately, so I wondered what this creature would smell like, feel like, sound like.

I started to see an angel. And not just any angel, mind you, I wanted something grand and majestic. So, I saw an archangel. Gabriel. The one who spoke the terrifying news to Mary, who delivered the Quran to Muhammad. The train pulled out of the station and this angel started coming into better focus.

The man in the tan jacket was still playing the game, the student was full asleep now, and as much as I wanted to start writing down my impression of an archangel standing next to my seat on this train, all I could think of was how my mother would never have let me highlight a book the way that woman across from me was doing. I could hear her voice clear in my head, saying to me, "We do not write in our books. Ever. Be careful with books."

And I thought of that old photograph of the two of us together at the lake; the one with just us, standing on the pier. I am small, wearing a blue satin swimsuit, holding my mother's hand. She was wearing a white dress and we are both looking at my dad, holding the camera.

And my First Communion. I am standing in line in the church and my friend Jean isn't feeling well. We all figure it's probably just nerves. And I am wearing my cousin's white dress. It's hidden underneath a white graduation gown that covered everything up – so that the poorer students in my class didn't feel left out if their families could not afford to buy them the white dress.

As I am recalling these events, these images, I notice the dark floor of the train has started to become light. There is a light rolling toward my feet the way fog rolls onto a stage in the theater when something otherworldly or mystical is about to happen. It's a saturated sunset peach and the gray and red flecked linoleum floor of the train car recedes until all I can see is that sunset peach.

The man in the tan jacket, the student with the red bag, and the woman with the yellow highlighter are fairly motionless and I notice the train has stopped in the middle of the tunnel, probably somewhere between Manhattan and Roosevelt Island.

The fluorescent overhead lights in the car are now dark, the walls and ceiling are shades of a midnight blue – the color of the twilight sky just before nightfall. And standing next to me is a slim figure with hair the color of freshly minted copper pennies, and he is wearing a long, white dress.

So I know I have to start writing – nothing this glorious can last and I want to remember everything. I pull out my notebook and start looking for my pencil, but I'm distracted by memories.

I'm in my living room at home and my dad is taking my picture. It's my junior prom and I'm wearing a white dress.

And I'm sitting in the auditorium, listening to high school graduation speeches. I'm surrounded by my friends and we're nervous and excited. Caps, gowns, flowers, parents, uncomfortable shoes, and under the white gown, I'm wearing a white dress.

Be not afraid.

No one looks up.

Be not afraid.

It's him. And he is talking to me. I am not afraid, but I am filled with memory.

I have my pencil now and I start writing quickly: sunset peach, midnight blue, white dresses and my mother is pouring champagne at my wedding. The guests are smiling at me and I'm standing behind a tall white cake with a glass in my hand.

As I write, the angel slowly raises his wings and they stretch out left and right until they fill the length of the train car and if I could reach out, I could touch his arm.

Everything is suspended as he stands there and I try to capture the images.

I write: copper colored hair, white gown, magnificent wings, the sound of his voice.

And I can taste my mother's Irish Soda Bread, warm from the oven, and the chill of her peach preserves. The kitchen faces the driveway where my father is standing, smoking a thin cigarette. He's wearing a white T-shirt. There are fresh-picked Lily of the Valley flowers on the table in a glass and I can smell new-mown grass and the gardenia cologne my mother wore because it reminded her of Ava Gardner.

The angel is lowering his wings and I realize I have not seen his face. As I set down my pencil, I look down at the floor. It's gray-flecked black linoleum now and the man in the tan jacket has finished his game, but as I look up to take in the details of the angel's face, he's gone.

The student is getting ready to leave the train, the

woman has put her highlighter away and I've got nothing if I do not have an image of the angel's face. I wanted to be David today, composing new psalms – but I hadn't even seen the angel's face.

I hear the conductor call the station stop.

I put my notebook away and drop my pencil into the bottom of my bag and I stand up to leave. There is the woman with the little girl that I saw when I first sat down. We walk to the escalator that takes us up to the landing and crosses over to the downtown platform. The little girl steps up next to me. I am filled with the memory of my childhood, my life. The mother is wearing a red T-shirt and jeans and she reaches out with both arms to caution the girl to hold the handrail and be careful on the stairs.

As the mother passes me, I can't see her face, but I get a look at her shirt as she walks out of the station and onto the street. Printed on the back was a pair of white angel wings.

The Two-Meter Relay

"Good afternoon, why don't you take a seat?"

The tall man in the navy blue suit and the classic club tie gestured toward the chair at the head of the table. Ashley Jean McDonald sat down, smiling, placing her resume on the table in front of her. She set her purse on the floor and quickly crossed her legs at the ankles and folded her hands in her lap. They teach you to do that in the pageant circuit.

"Thanks very much. I'm very happy to be here," she nodded toward the man. He picked up the papers and started reading out loud to her.

"So, Miss McDonald, I see you've got a degree from Harvard. That's good, that's very good."

Ashley Jean leaned forward. "Yes, Phi Beta Kappa." She pointed toward the papers in his hands.

"And I see you were a cheerleader for the football team in high school. You don't see that so much on resumes anymore."

She grinned. "Oh, I know what people say. They say that cheerleaders are not really smart and they're just the popular girls, but you should know I organized three bikini car washes and 19 bake sales to earn money to visit our state capital and meet with the governor for the day."

"Interesting, interesting. And I see you tutored Puerto Rican children in the flood zone over your spring breaks in college?"

Ashley Jean bobbed her head quietly. "That was such a great and rewarding experience for me. To be able to bring American values to those poor children living in those huts near the beach." She pulled a neatly folded Kleenex out of her bag and started to dab her eyes in the corners so as not to smear her eye liner.

"I see." The tall man turned to the second page.

"So, how do you feel you will fit in here at Coleman, Field, Dabney, and Marshall?"

He folded his hands and rested them on her resume.

She took a sip of the water in her glass.

"I feel I will fit in here with all the honest people here who are doing hard work to represent the wrongly accused, to see to it the man on the street has a strong ethical advocate. I will work very hard to make sure everyone can place their trust in me and know I will act with complete discretion and confidentiality."

Ashley Jean felt satisfied that she'd really hit the nail on the head with that answer. She could already see herself getting off the bus with her little paper bag full of breakfast, wearing her clean, white running shoes, carrying her Manolos in her bag.

"May we contact your previous employer?"

"Oh, why, yes, of course. You can call this number here and speak with Mrs. McDonald. She's my moth-, sorry, she's my mentor."

She pointed to the listing at the top of her resume.

"Just one last question," he said. "It says here you competed in the 2012 London Summer Olympic Games. That must have been very exciting to win a gold medal in the Two-Meter Relay."

Ashley Jean was undaunted.

"I felt very proud to represent my country. It was the thrill of a lifetime to see the American flag being raised and to hear *America the Beautiful* over the loudspeakers. My family was very proud and all my friends were there."

Ashley Jean shifted her weight in her chair and waited for the tall man to respond.

"Well, I think we're done here. It was lovely to meet you."

He stood up and tucked her resume into a black leather folder and slid his pen into its little side pocket.

Ashley Jean picked up her purse and offered her hand to the tall man to shake his hand and then, be on her way. He declined the offer and placed the folder under his arm.

He confided in her, "You know, of course, there's no Two-Meter Relay in the Olympics, right? That's only a little more than 6 feet. I think my dining room table is longer than that."

Ashley Jean looked down and started drawing small circles on the shiny surface with her index finger.

"And you know, of course, they don't play *America the Beautiful*, they play the National Anthem, right? And Puerto Rico is part of the United States. They are Americans, too."

She looked up at him for an instant and then back down at the table.

"Probably not Phi Beta Kappa either, right?"

She blurted out, "Does this mean I don't get the job?"

He squinted at her, scanning her face. "I don't know. What about the degree from Harvard?"

Ashley Jean straightened up. "My B.S.?"

"Was it?"

"BS?"

Ashley Jean picked up her purse and turned toward the door with a shrug.

"Uh huh."

She tried one more time.

"Does it count that I *watched* some of the Olympics on TV when they were in London?"

The tall man opened the door for her. She gave him a half smile and walked out of the room, letting him ring the elevator for her. She took her lip gloss out of her bag and dabbed a bit, calculating that she had just enough time to get a coffee at Sarabeth's Kitchen before her next interview.

At the Harvard Alumni Club in midtown.

The Real Space Man

He always hated occasions like this, but Jim hoped today would be different. After all, he'd already done the whole parade plus speeches bit before, what was it, maybe 20 times? It was just the damn kids' questions they insisted he answer, the Kids Quiz. He hated lying to the kids.

"Jim, sweetie, don't forget your little flag pin," Jo Ann called from the kitchen.

"Got it!" Jim shouted back. Jim met Jo Ann in the kitchen. "Let's get this over with already."

Jo Ann brushed some lint off his lapels.

"I never should have let that gas station kid think I'd been to outer space with NASA."

JoAnn picked up her pocket book.

"Look, we both know you don't really look all that much like Neil Armstrong, but if these nice people want to think you're an astronaut, we're not going to burst their bubble today, alright?"

Jo Ann drove downtown. The fire chief was standing next to the mayor on the corner of the supermarket parking lot.

"Here he comes, folks. It's our space man!"

One fire truck, two ambulances, all three police cars, and two shiny new convertibles were ready to go. The high school marching band had already started toward Third Street where they'd turn onto Main.

"This car's for you, sir," said a nice young man. Jim got in the back seat, nodding. Jo Ann parked the car and then got in beside him. The driver started off toward the marching band.

"Don't you love a parade, sir?" asked the nice young man. "Very pleased to meet you," he added.

On Main Street, they could see the crowds lining the curb, taking little movies. When the car got to the high school, the driver pulled right out onto the football field. The nice young man jumped out, opened the car door for Jim and

Jo Ann, and the crowd roared. The Mayor had already taken his place next to the microphone.

"Ladies and gentlemen, children of all ages," the Mayor shouted into the mike, quickly covering his ears, the electric feedback drowning out his greeting.

"It is my distinct honor and privilege to present a real live American hero!"

Everyone shouted and clapped, pushing their kids closer to the podium, cameras in hand to get the shot with Jim.

"Today, we're going to start with the Kids' Quiz for the anniversary of the moon landing. Could you step up to the mike please? Kids, get ready to talk to a real space man."

A timid 4th grader started the ball rolling.

"Mister? What was it like to walk on the moon?"

Jim clenched his teeth and smiled at him, "It looked real scary, didn't it? Next?" he added quickly.

A young girl stepped up.

"Mister? What was it like seeing the earth out the window of the space ship?"

"Those pictures you've seen don't lie, kid. Next?"

The girl stepped aside, adjusting the microphone for her younger sister.

"Mister? How come you don't wear a space suit?"

Jim covered the mike with his hand and leaned over to Jo Ann. "I can't keep doing this, Jo." She put one finger across her lips.

"Well, missy, about that suit," Jim started. "Let me tell you the truth."

Today was the day – finally. It was time to come clean and let everyone know he had never been on an Apollo mission, had never won a medal, and he wouldn't know the way to Cape Canaveral without a map. Jim felt great. He felt liberated. And he'd let them know he was just the guy who mowed the lawn and raised the American flag every day for the high school.

Mbeep.

Everyone looked up.

Mbeep, mbeep.

The sky got dark, like it was clouding over. Then there was a deafening, whirring sound.

Hovering overhead, there was a spinning, silver, Frisbee-shaped space ship whirring and beeping, then zap!

Mbeep, it was gone.

And so was Jim.

I knew it was only a matter of time before they came back for him, Jo Ann thought to herself.

She leaned over to the nice young man who sat there stunned, silent. She asked if the nice young man could please take her back to her car.

In the end, Astronaut Jim Stone didn't need to come clean to the kids about NASA or the view of the earth out the window of a space ship.

Apparently, he didn't need a space suit either.

Collecting Days

Today is Monday, today is Monday
Monday, string beans Tuesday,
spaghetti Wednesday, soup
Thursday, roast beef
Friday, fresh fish
Saturday, chicken
Sunday, ice cream
*All you hungry children, we wish the best to you!**

Dottie started buying the newspapers the day after her sister Carol died.

I just wanted to make a scrapbook, she told everyone, *a scrapbook with all of Carol's write-ups in it. I don't know what all the fuss is about. It's just a few newspapers, after all.*

Dottie kept them in stacks, so one day, when she was ready, she'd make Carol's scrapbook.

It started innocently enough, didn't it? Just stacks of newspapers, sorted by day, then by week, then by month.

Everything neat and tidy.

I'll just be going out now, she told everyone, *out to the newsman on the corner. Be right back!*

And the papers piled up, very neat and tidy.

Dottie bought the magazines too. Not the sports ones or the ones that the men looked at.

I'll just be picking up those fan magazines. You know, the ones about the Hollywood stars? It's my collection. I need Tuesday to be complete, after all. And the newsman is very kind. It's like he knows what I want before I ask him for it.

Hello? Dottie picked up the phone that sat on top of Tuesday.

Hello? There's nobody there, she told the phone that never rang anymore. *Now, who would call?*

Hello? Hello? And it became a routine.

Everyone finds comfort in a routine, she told everyone. *I like things neat and tidy.*

So, next to Tuesday, Wednesday sat. Thursday's pile stacked up next, neatly. And there were codes too.

"All you hungry children, I wish the best to you!"

On Monday, Dottie shopped for string beans. Monday's paper, Monday's Hollywood stars, Monday's string beans, and can after can of beans came into the house to take its place. Just in case, there were cans of string beans. Dottie wouldn't want to go hungry on Monday.

On Tuesday, spaghetti. Cans of spaghetti, all alike, stacked in piles next to the Tuesday papers, and so on to make the week. She made space in the refrigerator for any extra roast beef, fresh fish, chicken. The Sunday ice cream piled up in the freezer so Dottie went over to the Tuesday pile and called Sears and Roebuck to ask them to deliver another freezer, just in case, and then filled it up too, piling the Sunday papers and the Sunday magazines right next to it. She left the tags on the freezer though, just in case.

Then Dottie started getting confused. Once the week was done, where could she put the next Monday if not in the pile of last Monday's things? Everything neat and tidy, Monday must go with Monday, week after week.

After a few months, Dottie's neat day piles stacked up to the top of her settee and slowly, so slowly she barely noticed, everything she had was consumed, swallowed up, just gone now under the piles of the days of the week.

So she made a narrow path and the path was neat and tidy, too. It was adequate at first, then smaller and smaller as it snaked down the hall, through the kitchen, into the dining room, and ended in the double parlor next to the new freezer from Sears. But it didn't stop there. The path was leading Dottie now, pulling her along, day after day, room after room. She would start on her path, visiting her days, one by one as she passed, and the path would carry her along.

It was hard to guess how many trips, back and forth, she would make on any given day, but it was many. Sometimes she would watch the moon rise out the windows in the double parlor, just past Friday, and she'd think to herself, Carol's really missing something now that she's gone.

Then, Dottie had to use the extra sections in her Sunday papers to cover up the windows. This was a comfort to her. They were starting to watch. They were always looking in, judging her. But once the papers were up and the lights were on, they all went away and she would watch the moon in peace through a tiny corner of glass where she couldn't reach with the Scotch tape.

The money held out, the newsman had every day's purchases ready for her, the paper hung neatly, hugging against the windows, Monday stacked on Monday, and she couldn't see them looking in anymore. The newspaper in the windows started to crack and yellow from the sun, but Dottie didn't notice really.

Dottie wasn't feeling well. She started to worry she might be dying like Carol. So, on Thursday, she decided to stop by the drugstore on her way to the newsman. She looked both ways and crossed the street at the corner. But something tugged at her arm suddenly and wouldn't let go.

Dottie argued, *Please let me go, I have to get drugs, or I'll die. Let me go!*

"Carol, no!" And it was too late.

Carol pulled her, pulled her away and suddenly, Dottie was gone, too.

For the next three weeks, the building people took apart Dottie's piles of days. They didn't know to start with Monday so they pulled and dragged willy-nilly until all her days were gone from her hall and her kitchen and her dining room, all the way into her double parlor where they found all the Sunday ice cream sitting in her freezer next to the settee.

When they were done, the real estate people moved in to stage the place for the sale. Someone mentioned it was haunted, but it wasn't really.

Now, it was just neat and tidy.

** It's a Kindergarten memory song – to remember which food goes with which day of the week in sequence.*

Getting Fresh Water in Your Goldfish Bowl

They say that goldfish brains are so small that each time the fish swim from one side of their bowl to the other, they think they've gone someplace new. They are content to explore the same few square inches of water because to them, since they don't remember where they've been, it's all fresh territory. Like a vacation.

City people are a lot like goldfish. We take the same bus, the same trains, we walk to the same deli for bagels and a small-coffee-milk-no-sugar every day but somehow, we are content because, just like the little-brained fish, we can find enough excitement to keep us swimming. We keep it familiar, but there's always something to remark about, something new to share over dinner.

Getting out of the city to recharge is something rich New Yorkers have done for centuries. We have country houses or a "house upstate," maybe a timeshare in the Hamptons where we can revel in the change of scenery and commune with nature for a short spell. It sounds idyllic. But to be fair, these more well-to-do folks tend to exchange one familiar fishbowl for another without ever really exchanging the confines of their city life with something truly unconfining out in nature. That would be scary.

The rest of us, the less well-to-do, lie around on a Sunday afternoon in Central Park or take in the Orchid Show at the New York Botanical Garden. The Cloisters in Fort Tryon Park is particularly lovely this time of year and the array of flowering trees in Riverside Park is not to be missed if you are trying to get closer to nature but your budget keeps you in town.

A few years ago, I decided to step completely outside every semblance of comfort zone life and tried hiking in the mountains. I needed to abandon my city routine, and although I may not be the traditional outdoorsy type, I do love to walk. I designated my son as traveling companion, we bought plane, train, and metro tickets, we tucked a couple of maps in our backpacks, and we took off. We flew from Paris to Toulouse, France where we spent a few days looking at medieval churches. That's what I do on vacations. I look at churches. Well, to be honest, churches and cemeteries. But then we took a local train to St. Jean Pied de Port in the French Pyrenees, traditionally the starting point of the Camino Francés, the Way of Saint James, which ends in northwestern Spain in the beautiful cathedral town of Santiago de Compostela. We spent one night in St. Jean before heading out on a twelve-hour hike through a famous mountain pass into Spain. We crossed the Pyrenees, taking the same route as Charlemagne, Napoleon, and Saint Francis of Assisi. By nightfall, we arrived in the Spanish region of Roland, the tiny village of Roncesvalles. The next morning, we hailed a cab into Pamplona and from there, we took a train on to Madrid and back into urban civilization again.

In that one extraordinary day in the mountains with my son, I learned a little something about nature. I watched other hikers stride on past me, smiling as if the climb was nothing they hadn't done many times before. I watched farmers leading their cows in and out of barns, hosing down the walkways. I saw sheep graze and birds swoop and the air was so clean it nearly made me cry. There were flowers everywhere and the most amazing inky black beetles crossing our path as we stepped gingerly over them. Near the end of the route, as we approached the town, we crossed through a pine forest and the path was bordered by thick thorn bushes. By this time of day, my son had gone on ahead and I had the path to myself. It was blissfully still.

It's embarrassing to admit that this hike was an adventure for me. I know people for whom this kind of trek would have been routine or uneventful, but for us, we were knocked out by the stunning views from the top of the mountains, looking down into the valleys. We were stunned by the way the breeze felt and the way the pine trees smelled of thick, fresh sap. When I got back to New York, I wanted to ask, did you know that sheep will walk right close by you if you don't frighten them? But I figured that everyone but me knew that already. Do you know how delicious cold mountain water tastes on a hot day? I'm used to water in those clear plastic bottles you keep in your bag or on your desk at work. In the end, I couldn't say much of anything because I didn't want my friends to think I was slow.

Even though I came back to the same apartment, the same job, the same deli for my bagel with coffee-milk-no-sugar, I knew the water in my bowl had changed. I'm still the same little-brained fish who can swim from side to side and still find something wonderful to do when I get there, but my frame of reference is much greater than it was before.

Don't get me wrong: I'm not tempted to experience nature by lying in the grass in Central Park because I'll break out. I'm allergic to grass. And I won't do that Polar Bear Club dip into the Atlantic out at Coney Island in January any time soon.

I have gone on other, much longer hikes in the mountains since that first trip with my son because now, I'm hooked. I think part of the allure of a trip like this is that it is both ephemeral and long-lasting at the same time. The event passes, but the benefits are there for a very long while. Everything seems less scary to me now because I can always say, "You know, I hiked across the Pyrenees from France into Spain through a mountain pass that Charlemagne and Napoleon used." And wherever I am, I can close my eyes and call up the way the cool breeze felt on my shoulders or the way the water from the fountains splashed my face. People were kind to us and we didn't get lost.

As I write this, it's late on a school night. I'm sitting in New York with CNN in the background, listening to my daughter talk on the phone and my son humming along with some music on his computer, and I am content because I am surrounded by the comforting sights and sounds of my home and everything is familiar. But I know that any day I choose, I can put on my shoes, grab my bag, and just walk right out the door into some new adventure in a completely familiar place.

Like Dorothy in *The Wizard of Oz* movie, I always had the keys, or rather shoes, I guess, to my own happiness. I just didn't know it.

You don't have to buy expensive property out in the country to get back to nature, but every so often, you should change the water in your bowl.

Walking to Church

When my parents moved into their first home, a gift from my great aunt, the one thing that my mother always said was the most significant consideration in choosing the location was that she be able to walk to church. When I was younger, I thought that was so unnecessary since we went one block to the grocery store in our car, six or eight blocks in the car to the bank.

Why was proximity to a church so important? I walked to church, I walked to the parish grade school, and I learned over time that it was less about walking and more about the feeling we got from being close to our church.

We were surrounded, growing up, with families who all wanted the same thing, to be able to walk to church. The fringe benefit, of course, which meant little to me as a child, was that you found the familiar, you found the similar, and you had comfort because you knew that on your way to church, you would meet friends and neighbors who would sit by you, who would sing Christmas carols with you, who would follow the Way of the Cross or recite the Rosary with you.

As I got older, and found myself traveling longer and longer distances to church, I found that the church meant less to me. I lived in Chicago for a while and attended a beautiful church where my mother's best friend, Betty, and her husband were married. I drove there and left right away, never going to the little coffee hours after Mass, but hurrying right home for lunch and the rest of my day. I honestly can't say I remember much of that church at all now, other than the street it was on. Distance did not improve the experience for me.

When I moved to New York, I couldn't even find a Catholic church in the neighborhood. I was now carless and in a position to walk everywhere and I thought of my mother and how vital proximity was to her. But my first church in New York was a famous one with a professional choir that I was fortunate to join. This was not a Catholic congregation but rather a sister church to one where I sang in Chicago for a time. I made friends right away, we shared cabs to and from the church and choir rehearsals, and after the midnight service on Christmas Eve, sometimes we'd wait for the longest time for a bus together in the cold. But I couldn't walk there. In those days, the neighborhood between the famous church and my apartment was not safe enough to walk through.

After the choir director left the famous church, I left too. I had children now and wanted to take them to a Catholic church. So I set out to find us a church and I found such a beautiful place, just at the edge of the diocesan cachement for the parish. This church is on a side street, it doesn't have a full professional choir, it's not famous, and when I refer to it, most people say, "Where is that exactly?" But it's my church now and it has become important.

When my children were growing up, they all attended Sunday School there and I sang off and on for a while as a cantor before joining the choir. The music director in those days was amazing: a WWII veteran who told stories of playing pianos during wartime church services. He improvised on the organ after the hymn tunes were done and I miss it now that he's retired and moved away. He had a way around the music that made seamless progressions from one piece to the next that created such a full and lovely background to the Mass. I never appreciated him so much as when he left. And it's not to say the new organist isn't wonderful, but it took him a while to find his way.

So I wonder if my mother ever realized what a profound effect her house hunting criteria would have on me? I have learned that it's not only in the walking or the familiar that you find a home in a church, it's in the church itself. Sometimes, you can sit in the back with the crying babies and get nothing out of the experience. Sometimes, those very babies are what enrich the experience for you. And sometimes, you just find the familiar, the similar, the comfort you thought were found simply by being in proximity to the church.

It's not the proximity or the walk, it's the people and the history and the life of a church itself that matter most to me. I take two trains or one bus and one train to this little church on the side street and have never felt so at home because there is mercy in this building, at this Mass, with these people I don't live anywhere near.

As for my mother, I never appreciated her so much as when she left.

About the Title

When I started searching for a way to title this collection of stories, I looked for a similar title to *A Marshmallow on the Bus*. I really wanted my second book to be of a similar appearance to the first. I thought, since the stories were selected in similar ways, written in similar places, the bus and the train, that I would continue the "on the MTA" description.

I had written in my first book about seeing many people praying on the train one Sunday and how reticent I would be about praying in public. That incident reminded me of saying the rosary with my family and I wondered how you could get comfortable praying on a subway train.

Prayer beads did not appear on the floor of a subway car the way a lone marshmallow appeared on the floor of my BX6 bus to Manhattan one morning. Rather, they stand in for all the curious things I see every day in the oddest places. What was it? The "incongruous things of life."

I love New York!

(Back cover photo credit: Grace Baird)

Walk down that lonesome road all by yourself,
Don't turn your head back over your shoulder.
And only stop to rest yourself when the silver moon
is shining high above the trees.

James Taylor, *That Lonesome Road*

89254712R00082

Made in the USA
Middletown, DE
15 September 2018